D0678288

WHAT'S GONE WRONG WITH DEVELOPING LEADERS

THOUGHTS ON MARY AND HER BOOK

These are changing times. Business is different than in the last decade. It's tougher. The days of leading your organization through change by using group training events and the "management fad of the week" are gone. Those things have their place, to be sure. But by themselves they are not enough initiate and sustain real change.

To engage your team in a meaningful way, you have to accept the fact that a multi-dimensional approach is required. This is not universally popular, for the obvious reason that it requires more from us as leaders. What does a multi-dimensional approach look like in this context? It means taking the time and effort to create a culture that fosters engagement.

You need a guide to help you on this journey—someone who has been down this path before you, who knows where the shortcuts and the pitfalls lie. Mary Hladio is such a guide. Not only does she have the benefit of extensive expertise, and not only does she have an impressive list of companies and clients on her resume . . . she has the results to back up her expertise.

I've known Mary for years, and I can tell you that she also possesses the most rare and valuable of business assets: unflinching integrity. Heed the wise words in this book, and use them to your advantage. You won't be sorry.

—**Ray Edwards**, Best Selling Author and Keynote Speaker

THOUGHTS ON LEADERSHIP

Leadership may be among the most needed and least understood elements in our world today. To paraphrase the great poet, "No one is an island." We all succeed with the cooperation and help of others. This success is only possible via leadership.

Leaders don't just make other people follow them and their vision, but instead, leaders attract and combine individuals whose collective visions move the leader's vision forward. When a leader's goal is met, the individual team members' personal goals should be met.

My friend Jim King, former NBA basketball player, shared with me, "A leader is a leader all the time." I have found this to be true in that real leaders never get a day off. You will be viewed as a leader when you become someone worth following. True leadership is more about who you are and what you do as opposed to rehearsed words that you might say.

I've always believed that you should never take advice from anyone who doesn't have what you want. In this way, leaders become people who can take others down a trail that the leader has already traveled or experienced. Within these pages, Mary Hladio tackles one of the most critical components of your success. You will begin to learn both how to be a leader and how to identify others as true and worthy leaders.

A great leader doesn't have to be perfect, but they do have to be consistent and focused. My mentor—the late, great legendary Coach John Wooden—often told his players, "You will be known for a lifetime of achievement or one weak moment of a moral lapse."

We have seen political leaders, sports figures, entertainers, and successful business people whom we admired lose their influence as a leader over one single personal failing. Becoming a leader is not a gimmick or an act you put on. It is, instead, the constant striving to be worthy of leadership.

I have written 30 books. Six of them have been turned into major motion pictures with two more in production. In each of my stories, I try to portray leaders as attainable human figures who have dedicated themselves to a worthwhile cause. Their dedication attracts others, and they become viewed as a leader.

When you read the last page of this book, you will not have ended your lesson in leadership, but you will be embarking on a lifelong quest of learning, growing, and striving to be the leader you were meant to be.

—**Jim Stovall**, Bestselling Author: *The Ultimate Gift*

WHAT'S GONE WRONG WITH DEVELOPING LEADERS

WHY TRADITIONAL LEADERSHIP TRAINING MISSES THE MARK

MARY HLADIO

NEW YORK

NASHVILLE • MELBOURNE • VANCOUVER

WHAT'S GONE WRONG WITH DEVELOPING LEADERS
WHY TRADITIONAL LEADERSHIP TRAINING MISSES THE MARK

© 2017 MARY HLADIO

All rights reserved. No portion of this book may be reproduced, stored in a retrieval system, or transmitted in any form or by any means—electronic, mechanical, photocopy, recording, scanning, or other,—except for brief quotations in critical reviews or articles, without the prior written permission of the publisher.

Published in New York, New York, by Morgan James Publishing. Morgan James is a trademark of Morgan James, LLC. www.MorganJamesPublishing.com

The Morgan James Speakers Group can bring authors to your live event. For more information or to book an event visit The Morgan James Speakers Group at www.TheMorganJamesSpeakersGroup.com.

ISBN 978-1-68350-223-4 paperback
ISBN 978-1-68350-224-1 eBook
ISBN 978-1-68350-225-8 hardcover
Library of Congress Control Number: 2016915220

Cover Design by:
Rachel Lopez
www.r2cdesign.com

Interior Design by:
Bonnie Bushman
The Whole Caboodle Graphic Design

In an effort to support local communities, raise awareness and funds, Morgan James Publishing donates a percentage of all book sales for the life of each book to Habitat for Humanity Peninsula and Greater Williamsburg.

Get involved today! Visit
www.MorganJamesBuilds.com

DEDICATION

I dedicate this book to my parents—all three of them.

First to my mother, whose encouragement not only fostered my entrepreneur spirit, she instilled a sense of purpose as part of her legacy. My Mother told me I would write a book one day.

To my "biological" father, who provided me with a sense of loyalty, adventure and travel, and to the father that raised me, who demonstrated devotion and leadership whether it was when he served our country, or as head of our family and as a member of the church.

Through thick and thin, including my years of rebellion, my parents shaped me into the person I am today. I learned a lot about leadership characteristics and how to influence people I work with from their example. While they are no longer with me on this Earth their spirit lives on—through me—and through my writing.

CONTENTS

ACKNOWLEDGEMENTS

To my Lord and Savior, who has blessed me with experiences and talents to write this book.

So many people have contributed to this book in one way or another. This book started out as outline and bullet points on a screen. There are people that cared enough to challenge me and hold me accountable to move into action. There are too many people to list by name here, but I appreciate you all and will forever be grateful.

To my loving husband, who has supported and grounded me, especially when my ideas were a bit out there. Never once did he doubt that I would complete this book.

To my knucklehead brothers for their counsel, humor and friendship through the years, as well as all my family members especially those that see the possibilities of success in their pursuits.

An accomplishment is rarely the result of one-person's endeavor, and the effort to bring this book into existence has been no easy task. It would not have happened without the motivation, coaching, coaxing, editing, and proof-reading from several people. I would like to call out a few:

Upon meeting Ray E and Joel C, my book blossomed from a concept and outline into something more; many thanks for helping me launch forward.

A special thanks to my assistant Jackie S, who keeps me organized and makes sure I stay on track in the business. She is my friend, sounding board, and even my taste tester.

This book would not have been completed if it was not for RM and her abilities to take my verbal rantings and help me form them into coherent expressions. A shout out to GS for his invaluable contribution in providing me with a fresh perspective as I rounded third and headed home to the finish. And in between there was Francois G, ever the contrarian, he was the first to read the final draft and provided his wonderful notes.

Thank you to David Hancock, Jim Howard, Megan Malone, Bethany Marshall, Nickcole Watkins and the rest of the team at Morgan James Publishing for publishing my book.

INTRODUCTION

I have one core mission in my work life: to ignite passion, pride, and effectiveness in organizations, leaders, and employees. Though this mission statement is short and sweet, it's not always easy. Many companies and managers fall back on the same old, same old when it comes to trying to develop effective leadership. That often translates to rolling out "training events" designed to try to manage broad areas that can't really be managed, such as change, time, and stress.

However, it takes more than a few "lunch and learn" initiatives to help organizations and individuals truly deal with the complexities of the workplace. The issues go far beyond standardized knowledge and training, so it's ineffective to slap on a "one size fits all" approach, such as those available through a "corporate university," standardized e-learning tools, or leadership training courses that have not been designed to address your company's specific challenges. In short: most of what passes today for leadership training and development just doesn't work.

How do I know that standard leadership development doesn't work? Just ask your employees. Employee engagement offers a reflection of your company's leadership, for better or for worse. A 2011 study on employee job satisfaction and engagement by the Society for Human Resource Management suggests that even if employees are satisfied with their jobs, that doesn't automatically translate into an engaged workforce.

The research showed that while a majority of employees (83 percent) are generally satisfied with their current positions, only 68 percent feel passion and excitement for their job, and just over half (53 percent) feel tuned in at work. That's a 30 percent drop-off between satisfaction and engagement.

To properly influence culture in a way that results in better engagement, you must first understand what true engagement would look like in your company. Real business success needs that optimal employee engagement, and that needs to be driven by the best leaders—and that's what this book is all about. You need to avoid falling into the trap of a "sheep dip" approach and rethink your approach to leadership development."

Once you see how all-encompassing the concept of culture really is, and what it takes to influence it at every stage of an employee's development to improve engagement, you can understand why it's so important for organizations to take a new approach to leadership development. By starting today to rethink your approach to training and development, you can begin to foster the type of effective leaders who, in turn, develop engaged employees that drive the health and productivity of your company.

To properly influence culture in a way that results in better engagement, you must first understand what optimal engagement would look like in your company. That's what this book is all about. Once you see how all-encompassing the concept of culture really is, and what it takes to influence it at every stage of an employee's development to improve engagement, you can understand why it's so important for organizations to take a new approach to leadership development. By starting today to rethink your approach to training and development, you can begin to foster the type of effective leaders who in turn develop engaged employees that drive the health and productivity of your company.

If your workforce isn't truly engaged in their work, then your company's approach to training isn't working. Effective, engaged leaders lead to effective, engaged employees that drive productive, healthy companies. In fact, separate research has shown that employee engagement is a force that drives overall performance outcomes, and is a leading indicator of a company's financial performance. Anything less than true engagement means your organization is failing to maximize its talent and potential.

However, if satisfaction doesn't equal engagement, then what does? The answer is: more than one thing. I refer to engagement as an über-dimension; in other words, a behavior that contains not just a single facet, but multiple ones. Trust, for example, is an über–dimension because within the concept of trust are many attributes and various levels. Trust can be given, and trust can also be earned; you can be trusting but not trustworthy.

The same is true for employee engagement. Engagement goes far beyond simply wanting your employees to be "happier at work." All aspects of a company's culture influence the level of engagement—or disengagement—of your employees. That includes everything from the corporate communication style, to employees' perceived level of influence within the organization and with customers, to the evaluation and review system, to everything in between.

In fact, engagement starts even before you hire someone. Engagement begins with the reputation of your company and its products and services, as well as the corporate role in the community. It continues with the recruitment and interviewing process. It includes understanding which behaviors are a good fit with your organization and which aren't, so that your managers can make smart hires and start off on the right foot.

Once someone is hired, the on-boarding and integration process during the first 60 to 90 days is vital to fostering positive engagement. So is the leadership team's ability to effectively communicate strategy and vision—and management's ability to translate and link to that strategy and vision in each department. In the end, it comes down not just to management, but to each and every person in the company helping to create a culture that encourages engagement rather than squelches it.

If you were to look up the definition of Leadership Development in Wikipedia, here's what you would find:

> ***Leadership development*** *expands the capacity of individuals to perform in leadership roles within organizations. Leadership roles are those that facilitate execution of a company›s strategy through: building alignment, winning mind-share and growing the capabilities of others.*

Read on though, and there is this somewhat compelling piece:

> *Classroom-style training and associated reading is effective in helping leaders to know more about what is involved in leading well. However, knowing what to do and doing what one knows are two very different outcomes; management expert Henry Mintzberg is one person to highlight this dilemma. It is estimated that as little as 15% of learning from traditional classroom-style training results in sustained behavioral change within workplaces.*

PART I

Why Most Leadership Development Doesn't Work

CHAPTER 1
MANAGING THE UNMANAGEABLE

Do you believe that developing your leaders can solve all of your company's organizational performance issues? Do you hope, like many other executives and entrepreneurs, that the answer is simply to "send them to a class—that will fix them"? This is just plain wrong. There are many issues and problems a business can face, and rolling out a generic training initiative is not always the answer. In reality, the approach that companies take to address any development effort is futile without it being tied to specific learning objectives that are relevant to *your* company and your company alone.

How often have I sat across the desks of small business owners or CEOs as they told me about employee turnover, communication challenges, and the struggle to hold people accountable for just doing their job? How often have I heard them describe how their business is stagnant—or maybe worse, their profits are down and operating costs are up? The answer is: more often than any of us would like to admit. Particularly disturbing is the fact that these concerns affect every aspect of these leaders' businesses, including customer service, quality, productivity, and overall effectiveness.

Yet despite these clear, comprehensive challenges, companies and managers often take the wrong approach to leadership development by focusing on trying to teach employees how to manage unmanageable aspects of their job. They champion predictable "training events" in a misguided attempt to help employees wrap their arms around problematic areas that match certain industry buzz words: change management, anyone? How about stress management, or time management?

Some things just can't be managed, and these programs aren't focused on the right things. For that reason alone, such training initiatives will not ultimately help companies reach their overall organizational goals in these areas. These programs also won't help to advance corporate growth strategy in any arena. How could they? The heart of these programs involves taking a solution from somewhere else without any consideration that your organization could have differences—even if they are minor—that render the strategies useless.

The bottom line is this: a two-hour module won't do it. In order to help employees truly deal with the challenges and complications of their work environment, you must go deeper and get more specific. These issues go far beyond what can be addressed by standardized knowledge and development tools promising quick-fix solutions.

WHY ONE SIZE FITS ONE

Every company is trying to solve a specific problem. What problem is your company trying to solve? The reason that most corporate training initiatives fail is that no one ever sits down to determine the answer to that question in advance. Without knowing what needs solving, training won't engage the correct problem-solving process. Your employees might be using techniques they've learned, but failing to apply them to the right problems.

Management expert Harold Stolovitch gets at this reality with his concept of "Telling Ain't Training." Most development efforts are simply exercises in "telling"—a facilitator talks at you about scenarios that are likely to be totally unrelated to your organization's unique issues. What should happen instead is that the "telling" needs to be transformed into connection, education, and application opportunities to develop customized activities that result in long-term behavior change.

To put it more simply, employees need the opportunity to be developed, not trained. You develop people; you train dogs. The difference is that while dogs are simply parroting back an action, people have the ability to apply their learnings to specific situations. You can't just "rinse and repeat" if your techniques aren't tied to a specific problem. Parroting back management principles—even if the principles are sound—won't get your company where you want it to go, but applying the right principles for your company will. Basic principles don't change much over time, but the application of those principles needs to be ever-changing to fit individual situations.

The application part of the leadership development puzzle is critical. I often tell teams I'm working with in this context that if they don't think I'm right then go apply it. Then come back and tell me that I'm wrong. I advise them to tie the technique to their specific problem, then "rinse and revise" until they get where they're trying to go. In truth, I hope that they do tell me I'm wrong—then we'll have a conversation that's based on what's actually happening. It's the dialogue that results from education and application that leads to true change. You need to assess what *truly* needs to be done, and then reinforce the learning.

Workshops aren't really the problem—the problem is that most workshops aren't designed with your company's issues in mind. They're one size fits all, when in reality, one size only fits one. What really needs to happen is that every workshop must be designed to address the problem that *your* company is trying to solve. Leadership development workshops should reflect a theme that's only meaningful to your company.

Here's a case in point:

One company that I worked with chose the theme "I'm Possible." The theme was not an "off the shelf" program, but one that emerged after several months of working closely with the company's management team to discover together what problem they were trying to solve.

This particular company had previously created a tradeshow initiative called "Follow Possible." The initiative had a two-pronged mission: to encourage potential customers to better understand certain innovative areas that the company was working toward, and to follow the possibilities of new strategies for future growth.

The "Follow Possible" theme resonated with employees because of the cultural references to the television series and movies that shared a similar name: "Mission Impossible." The theme evoked a sense of teams working together to overcome difficult challenges and unlikely odds, so we decided to leverage this commonality to address the company's specific challenges.

Because of the company's successful history with "Follow Possible," the "I'm Possible" theme offered a catchy way for senior management to capture the spirit of current initiatives while spinning it into something new. By morphing the feeling of "Impossible" to "I'm Possible," the company was able to provide employees with a sense of self-empowerment and possibility. It was the right choice for this particular management team, because it brought together their unique corporate history around a theme that was already familiar to employees, yet the revised spin made it fresh and relevant, Mission Impossible style.

Here's another example:

A new CEO came to the helm of a company that was struggling with revenues, employee morale, and community perception. The CEO recognized the potential within the organization, but needed a way to harness the power of employees and managers alike. There was only one problem: while they were a clinical organization focused on the mission of helping people, they were failing to act like a revenue-generating one.

What was needed were leaders who would actively embrace change within the company. This company did not need generic initiatives about change management, but a series of leadership development workshops designed to spur people to action in the context of what that organization was all about.

The resulting program was called "LEAP"—"Leaders Execute and Perform"—with the mantra: "You can't jump a chasm in two small steps—it takes a LEAP!" All leadership development efforts were inextricably linked to the specific initiative that this company was trying to solve: management recognized that it would take a leap of faith to get to a new direction.

Both the "I'm Possible" and "LEAP" themes told stories that worked for these particular companies—and these companies alone. The concepts behind these themes will never exist again in the same way for any other organization, because there will never be the identical players, barriers, and conditions that brought these themes to life. You need to find a way to do the same, but differently—that's the only way that your company can hope to manage the unmanageable.

CHAPTER 2
TEN MYTHS ABOUT DEVELOPING LEADERS

Part of the problem for companies trying to find solutions to organizational performance issues is that the promised value of generic leadership development programs has been accepted by corporate decision makers. Generalized programs are sold under the premise that they hold the key to whatever ails any company, regardless of each company's unique circumstances.

To understand the problem with buying into this erroneous belief, you must first understand the difference between what you may have been told about standardized training programs and the reality of them. Let's debunk ten of the most popular myths about common training programs.

MYTH #1: WHAT WORKS FOR GE OR DISNEY WILL WORK FOR YOU

A cookie-cutter approach to developing your employees that assumes what works somewhere else, like GE or Disney, will work for your company is never going to work. The same applies to the "big-box" training providers with 50 to 100 course libraries packaged ready to roll out and "fix" every imaginable management challenge for every size and type of business – they just don't work either. How do you know that you even need the boxed competencies—which by the way are very broad and lack specificity—if you haven't done your homework to find out what problem you *really* need to solve?

There's nothing that you can buy in a box, or in a canned speech or generic workshop, that will work for every company—no off-the-shelf program is ever going to fit. Whatever problems Disney had when they developed their solutions are not the same problems that your company is facing—and Disney's problems are different than GE's. The culture, the management, the employees, and the specific business model used in your company all make your challenges unique. Why wouldn't you need unique solutions as well?

MYTH #2: TRAINING CAN FIX HIRING MISTAKES

It can't. If a person isn't a good fit for a position, training isn't going to help. Hiring managers often gravitate toward hiring people like themselves. They are looking for a "mini-me" instead of thinking about what qualities represent the right skill set for the position. This is a hiring mistake that training can't fix.

Here's an example: I spoke with a CEO recently who was complaining about two account people he had hired. He needed problem-solving strategic thinkers, yet his new hires didn't excel in these areas. When grilled further, the CEO revealed that he had not asked one strategic question during the interviewing process—he had asked for information that could easily be found on a resume. He didn't ask what the candidates' actual responsibilities were versus others on their teams—he focused more on the interviewees' tone of voice and whether they had experience working with clients.

In short, he was more concerned with hiring someone like him than with finding the right competencies and skill sets for the job. The CEO did not interview these candidates for the qualities that he actually needed for the position. This was a hiring mistake—you don't want to start off with the wrong people in your key positions and then expect training to fix it.

MYTH #3: TRAINING CAN FIX PROBLEMS WITH COMPANY CULTURE, MISTRUST IN THE LEADERSHIP TEAM, OR ISSUES WITH STAFFING LEVELS AND WORKLOAD

These issues reflect underlying corporate principles that need to change—band-aid solutions in the form of training won't work. Company culture is a broad issue that requires management to fully understand how it's presently affecting employees in order to change it.

If the staff mistrusts the leadership team, then the problem needs to be fixed at the grassroots level—education is needed to understand this, not training. Imbalances in staffing levels or workload reflect cultural problems, and the solutions to these problems are individual to each company. Management must understand the reasons behind problems in these areas to solve them appropriately. Simply trying to apply general training principles to your teams, without getting to the bottom of what has caused these problems in the first place, will be ineffective and a waste of money.

MYTH #4: THERE IS A COURSE TOTO MAKE AN UNHAPPY, DISENGAGED EMPLOYEE OR A DYSFUNCTIONAL TEAM TURN THE CORNER OVERNIGHT

Harvard Business School professor and world-renowned change expert John Kotter recommends an eight-step change process in his book, *Leading Change*. Whether or not your company agrees with Kotter's specific steps, just looking at the types of actions that are involved in truly making change in an organization helps to reinforce the point that current training programs are unrealistic.

Kotter recommends creating a sense of urgency, recruiting powerful change leaders, building a vision and effectively communicating it, removing obstacles, creating quick wins, building on your momentum, and anchoring the changes in your corporate culture. Do you think a 90-minute module can effectively address all of these areas?

MYTH #5: EFFECTIVE TRAINING CAN BE A SINGULAR EVENT THAT IS SQUEEZED IN OVER A LUNCH HOUR

True leadership development is a much longer process, which as noted above has many steps that take time to address on a corporate level. Simply expecting your leaders to learn general strategies on the fly won't fix anything—even if some of the ideas have merit—and that's because it's the *application* of the strategies that matters.

When management training is reduced to a group Lunch and Learn, it's the application that's missing. When this happens, employees return to their desks after lunch, but have no concrete way to apply what they've learned to their specific situations. They're not empowered to problem solve. Unless you are taking the time to understand your managers specific challenges, proposing custom-fit solutions, and showing them how to apply them right there and then, they're better off just taking a regular lunch break.

MYTH #6: TRAINING IS MEANT TO FIX PEOPLE

"Fix it!!" This is something I hear repeatedly from small business owners and CEOs: "Just fix my people; I don't care how you do it." This often results in the "Flavor of the Month" approach to training that's become commonplace in Corporate America. But true development is not meant to fix people. In fact, people don't need fixing—processes and broader "work environments" do.

I'll give you an example. Research has shown that communication problems are at the root of 80 percent of problems at work. Therefore, companies often want their employees to learn how to communicate better to resolve team conflicts. However, many companies go about trying to find a solution in the wrong way when they simply provide training in communication skills. The concepts provided in standardized training are too broad—you have to break down the issue to discover its source.

The important question to ask is: what caused the communication breakdown? When you actually talk to each member of the team, it's clear each person knows how to communicate just fine. It's not anyone's individual communication style that needs fixing. It's understanding how to adapt and connect with other team members' specific communication styles that's the problem. The people involved aren't broken, but the overall process is—or as communications expert Steven Gaffney says: "The fish isn't sick. The water's dirty." Cleaning the water goes back to education and application.

MYTH #7: HOW THE TRAINING IS DELIVERED CAN MAKE A DIFFERENCE IN THE OUTCOME

You'll often hear companies and consultants debate about which training style is better. Instructor-led training? On-the-job training? How about the distance learner option or e-training? There are countless permutations of delivery methods, but guess what? None make a substantive difference in the *effectiveness* of the training.

You could request that leadership training be delivered on the moon while participants stand on their heads, but if the training methods aren't tailored to solve your company's specific problems, it will all be a waste of time. If your employees aren't clear about exactly how to apply the training to their own situations, then it won't help you to solve your organization's performance issues.

MYTH #8: WHO DELIVERS THE TRAINING CAN SOLVE YOUR PROBLEMS

Some companies get star struck by the idea of bringing in a big-name speaker. While it may be nice to have a Seth Godin or a Daniel Pink provide a kickass keynote speech in the name of providing employees with training opportunities, it won't solve your problem.

Are you starting to see a theme developing here? How can you expect that a speaker, whether named Malcolm Gladwell or Santa Claus, who has never set foot in your organization, has met none of your people, and knows none of your corporate challenges and goals to be able to solve *your* company's problems?

MYTH #9: THE LOGISTICS AROUND THE TRAINING CAN ENHANCE THE VALUE OF THE LEARNING

Management teams often go to great lengths to set up what they think will be just the right training experiences for their people. Some leaders go nuts over the idea of designing off-sites, retreats, weekend workshops, and other types of bonding experiences for their teams. Some think that giving training first thing on Monday, or on a Friday afternoon, will do the trick.

Unfortunately, though planning such events may be fun, the location, day, and time of the training don't necessary enhance the value of the learning—in fact, they can detract from it. If there are too many bells and whistles, employees may pay more attention to the frills than the substance. While your heart is in the right place in wanting the experience to be comfortable, the truth is that what's comfortable for one person is different than what's comfortable for another. Some people may love sitting in a circle under a tree, while others will hate it and just want to get out of there.

MYTH #10: TRAINING IS A SECRET FORMULA THAT WITH THE RIGHT MIX WILL CURE ALL OF YOUR BUSINESS CHALLENGES

This all-encompassing myth is the biggest problem of all. There is no secret training formula that can be plugged into every work group to solve challenges. Training might be one component of the solution, but it's definitely not a cure-all. Instead, the answer lies in a much more considered approach:

- Taking a good long look at your organization and its underlying problems that no one wants to talk about;
- Taking the time to define the future state of your organization
- Thinking about what skills, behaviors, and culture are needed for future growth;
- Developing truly customized solutions for your company.

In summary, the issues you're seeking to resolve did not happen overnight, and it's going to take more than a two-hour or day-long workshop to move beyond the current challenges. You need to truly understand what's going on inside your organization in particular before you can determine how best to fix it.

When it comes to improving leadership development, many companies are stuck in a rut. Corporate environments often promote the belief that traditional leadership training is the only way to address organizational performance issues. But, as we've discussed, it doesn't work to lift a "best practice" process directly from another company, because it hasn't been tailored to your own employees' issues.

There's a better way and that is about leaving classic "training" behind, focusing instead on the much broader development of the competencies, skills, and behaviors needed for effective, authentic leadership, and here's something that's not a myth: you can do that through understanding and influencing company culture.

Culture change provides the bridge and connection to problem solving. Company culture is a multifaceted concept. Culture is organic and not static and so influencing it takes more than an overly broad, one-off training event.

CHAPTER 3
WHY YOU CAN'T MANAGE CHANGE

When we drill down into the specifics about why most leadership development doesn't work, we will invariably arrive at one conclusion: Certain types of challenges are inherently unmanageable. We've touched on some of the primary "unmanageables" already, but now let's really try to understand why training events that are focused on these specific areas are a waste of time, money, and staff resources.

"Change" is one of the biggest red herrings to human resources departments and corporate managers in search of quick fixes to organizational problems. Because so many aspects of work revolve around constantly changing circumstances, the prospect of lassoing it all up into a manageable process—capped by a tidy bow—sounds both ideal and appealing. Someone is offering training in change management? Sign us up! Sorry, but that's just a waste of time.

Basing your leadership development around the promise of change management is never going to work and people are foolish to think that it will. That's because there is no way that your company can actually "manage" change, no matter how many training exercises your employees and management team participate in. Research supports this assertion by suggesting that between 60 percent and 90 percent of change management initiatives either fail or fall short of expectations.

Here are just a few examples:

- The Wharton School of Business reports that according to research by IBM, while 83 percent of CEOs expect their companies to undergo substantial change, almost 60 percent cite failure with previous change initiatives.
- Forrester Research cites a 70 percent failure of change management initiatives.
- The *Journal of Cambridge Studies* (*JCS*) notes that the management literature contains countless examples of managerial failure when it comes to strategies involving organizational change and development. For example, a study by researchers Schaffer and Thompson found that out of 300 U.S. electronics companies surveyed, nearly 65 percent failed to reach improvements in quality following change management initiatives, and 90 percent of these programs were unsuccessful.
- In Europe, *JCS* notes a similar trend: despite more than two thirds of the top 500 companies introducing a change management initiative, only 8 percent of the managers in these companies believe that that the initiative was successful.

- European think tank *Project Smart* reports that a U.K. survey of government transformation programs found 65 percent of these to be unsatisfactory.

There's more to these trends than just numbers. Wharton points out that these change-initiative failure rates represent "lost opportunities, strained budgets, and a discouraged workforce."

BEHIND THE MYTH OF CHANGE MANAGEMENT

There are many reasons for these wholly disappointing statistics in the change-management arena, but they all link back to a primary truth: The way that most companies approach change is fundamentally flawed. An internet search around a definition of "change management" reveals the following being used on many different occasions; the bold emphasis is my own:

> *"A structured approach to shifting/transitioning individuals, teams, and organizations* ***from a current state to a desired future state."***

That's all well and good as the approach that many companies take to change management, but the problem is that they view change as a single discrete event. The implication behind this is the false belief that an organization can simply move from "here" to "there"—from one side that represents "change-related problems" to another side that represents "freedom from these problems."

The reality, as anyone who has managed in the corporate world knows, is that the process of navigating organizational change is nowhere near that straightforward. It's not the type of situation where "A + B = C." If you had to put a formula to it, it might look more like "A + B + C + D + E + F + G + H = X (where 'X' is unknown)."

I have suggested that we use A through H on the left side of the equation, instead of just A and B, because experiencing organizational change, whether you're an employee or a manager, is incredibly complex. It can't be managed through simple training initiatives; it can't be viewed as an A plus B.

Okay I've suggested eight letters in this hypothetical equation as a "hats off" to John Kotter and his eight-step change model, but it's possible that your company might require more letters or possibly less to accurately reflect what needs to happen to address organizational change. Your company might need "A + B… + P" or "A + B… + L" or "A + B… + F." but the point is not which formula is best, but that *each company requires its own formula.*

No one can give you a detailed breakdown of what you'll need in advance, without first taking the time to explore and examine your company's unique situation. As discussed in Chapter 1, leadership development, including a response to organizational change, should not be approached as a "one size fits all." The specific circumstances surrounding what needs to change are what should drive management's efforts to handle those issues, and not what some external facilitator has determined qualifies as "change management" for any and every organization.

That aside, you may wonder why I've suggested that the right side of the hypothetical change equation above results not in a known quantity, but in "X (where 'X' is unknown)." If you work through the steps that are appropriate for your specific company and don't follow someone else's generic training manual, shouldn't you at least end up with a specific, logical, and predictable result?

The answer is no. The nature of change is organic, not static. Change isn't a place that you finally reach with all of your problems solved. The place where your company's employees and managers will land, after completing the steps agreed for your own change, isn't the same spot that others who followed the very same steps would arrive at. That's because every organization and its culture are unique.

So the equation results in "destination unknown" for everyone, but that doesn't mean there isn't value in taking an organizational development approach to change, rather than a straight training approach. By taking the time to understand the full process of change and confront it with original, company-specific solutions, you can build the proper foundation for corporate transition and revision that leads to new opportunities, engaged employees, and an improved bottom line.

UNDERSTANDING THE PROCESS OF CHANGE

Now that we've seen why you can't manage change, let's see what you *can* do to help facilitate change in your organization and the simple answer is this: When you shift from a focus on "change management" to "change leadership," a whole new world of possibilities open up for your teams and your company.

So what's the difference between "change management" and "change leadership"? Though they may sound similar, this difference is quite fundamental. Lest you think this distinction is little more than a quibble over semantics, I encourage you to consider the following:

What many companies do when confronted with change is attempt to minimize the distractions that the change causes. Traditionally, companies will bring in an outside facilitator to provide a set of basic (non-customized) tools or processes, with the misguided hope of keeping the impact of change under control.

This is change management at its finest—designed to keep managers and employees from being negatively impacted by change, rather than to help them prosper and flourish as a result of change. Now you may be thinking, "What's wrong with trying to control change and prevent teams from being negatively impacted by it?"

Well the answer is that while on the surface these may seem like noble goals, remember the "non-customized" part. Off-the-shelf solutions designed with no specific company in mind (or perhaps based on what's worked for other mega-companies like GE or Disney) are really one size fits none. Your goal is to use an approach where one size fits one—and that is where *change leadership* comes in.

As you may have guessed from the differences implied by the words "management" and "leadership," there's another major distinction between these terms when the word "change" is in front of them. Change leadership represents a more comprehensive and visionary approach.

We can turn to Kotter again for perspective when he describes change leadership as "the driving forces, visions, and processes that fuel large-scale transformation." He explains that compared to the ideas behind change management, change leadership is, "much more associated with putting an engine on the whole change process, and making it go faster, smarter, more efficiently." In other words, change leadership involves macro-changes in your organization, and provides a more active approach than merely trying to minimize its effects.

In order to take this overarching, forward-thinking approach, you must figure out the best way to address the specific changes that are happening to your employees or your business. Notice I say "address" these changes, not "manage" them. You can address change, you can cope with change, and you can handle change—in fact, the ability to do so in today's constantly changing world is a critical skill set in work and life—but you can't manage it. Here are some ideas you might consider:

- *Address* change by leading a change initiative through effective communication;
- *Handle* change by talking to employees and trying to understand what the issues are within your specific company before introducing any development initiatives whatsoever;

- Working with employees to help them *cope* with change by ensuring that they have the information they need to operate effectively in their new environment.

In fact, these types of crucial communication steps should take place before making any decisions about the overall strategy for change leadership in your company, and which specific processes and tactics to use. Any change initiative is going to be more successful when your leaders get their teams to buy into what you are seeking to do.

In fairness, I must warn you that effective change leadership usually involves stepping outside of corporate comfort zones. You can't lead well from inside the box and you could well need to take risks. While the process may not feel as smooth and comfortable as simply putting your employees through the paces of standard training modules that promise quick-fixes, the chance for reward, real results, and lasting innovation is much greater.

REAL RESPONSE TO CHANGE

What does organizational change look like in real life? There are a couple of primary ways that companies (via the leadership team) and contributors (via employees) respond to change—whether they are initiating it or are the recipients of change initiatives. Understanding these responses can help further distinguish why the concept of change management is a fallacy, and why change leadership is what's really needed.

Change Initiators

Let's start with companies. Most companies are the instituters of change. Typically, a CEO or leadership team will spearhead a particular change and announce a move in a new direction. In other words, the senior management team has already completed their thinking and made their decision and that's: "This is now the direction that we're moving in as a company."

What is left to manage, since the change-related decision process is already over and done with? All that's left to manage is the communication effort related to the change, not the change itself.

Sure enough, when it comes to coaching companies most courses that dub themselves "change management" focused, with three key areas: communicating the vision, combating resistance to change, and sustaining change. Umm…what is it that's actually being managed here? There is nothing in most change management courses that talks about managing the change itself.

Still not convinced? Let's dissect the process a bit further. I challenge you to find a change management course that doesn't look something like this (which you'll see includes nothing about actually managing change):

The first thing a change management course geared at company leadership generally asks the team to do is come up with a vision for the change, and work on getting buy-in for that vision. Once you've come up with a vision, such courses will focus on helping the team to learn how to share the vision, providing context to employees about why the change is being made.

The course might spend time detailing how different employees are likely to react to the news: some will be positive, some will be hesitant but will move forward, and others may actually start working against you either visibly or behind the scenes. So the next course advises the leadership team on how to deal with this potential resistance to change.

Finally, most change management courses end with a focus on how management can sustain the change and make it the new norm. It might suggest ways to create an environment where there is no other option but the change, a la explorer Hernán Cortéz, who set out to conquer Central America and ordered his troops to burn the boats after landing in Mexico, removing all options to retreat and thus paving the way to victory.

Vision statements, sharing the vision, dealing with resistance, sustaining change…this sounds an awful lot like communications training to me, and then there's the fact that many trainings that are dubbed as "change management" are really nothing more than communications courses by a different name.

Change Receivers

What about employees, though—can't they learn how to manage the change that comes at them? Not really, so let's think it through. Say you're an employee who just got an announcement that your organization is about to change: maybe you're getting a new boss, or a different reporting structure, or your department is merging with another one. What will your process be for coping with that change?

It's basically just the flip side of what management goes through in relation to change. First, as an employee, you need to understand the change and what it means to you. That brings us back to the same points I just mentioned above—some will embrace the change, some will be on the fence until they learn more about it, and some will throw up roadblocks in an attempt to actively resist the change.

Just as is true of the leadership team, you can't manage change as an employee because there is nothing for you to manage—what's done is done. Trying to manage this kind of change as an employee is akin to getting stuck in traffic on the way to an important meeting. You can't manage what's going on with the traffic; you just have to go with the flow.

Of course, there are ways to *address* the change, *handle* the change, or *cope* with the change, but these strategies aren't managing the change.

The change has happened to you—you're stuck in traffic, or you have a new boss, or your company is merging. How you choose to respond to it is up to you.

In the case of traffic, whether you respond calmly or with road rage will determine how you feel during the experience. In the case of a new boss, whether you respond with enthusiasm or with resistance will determine whether you move with the organization, or move yourself out of it.

In any of these examples, whether you're the initiator of change as part of the leadership team or if change happens to you as an employee, you certainly have a choice to determine what you're going to do next. But in none of these examples is there a management component.

STEPS AND STAGES, NOT STRICT STRUCTURES

As you can see from the scenarios above, change management is not structured like project management. Projects can be managed, and as such, project management is a much more straightforward "A + B = C" equation. I have a project (A), you'll manage it (B), and we'll move toward a result that we both agree to (C).

Most project management courses reflect this by providing you with tools to help you manage specific projects. Note the difference between this straightforward match of project management courses with project management tools, versus what happens in change management courses.

In so-called change management courses, you receive tools either to communicate, handle resistance, or sustain new processes. Those are three different skill sets that have nothing to do with the change itself, because they would be necessary regardless of whether or not a particular change was happening.

Additionally, as discussed above, there's generally a longer equation to represent the steps and stages involved in moving through the process of change, and not all of these steps are equal. For management to lead change—which in essence boils down to helping employees deal with current or upcoming organizational changes—the leadership team needs to understand the entire process of change and how to deal with it efficiently.

And what does that involve? It all comes back to the big three mentioned above: communication, overcoming resistance, and sustaining change.

A Personal Example: Communication

When I joined a large medical device manufacturer as a manager, I came on board in the midst of sweeping corporate change. What did I do? You can bet that I didn't book a change management course to address it.

One of the first things I did was to write up my vision of what I thought the organization should look like. I took it to my boss and got his buy-in, then took it to the people who reported to me and got their buy-in. Then we presented that to the larger group and said, "Here's the vision."

Although this may sound similar to the "create a vision" step mentioned earlier that many change management courses feature as part of their curriculum, the difference is that my strategy requires no course or training—just common sense and effective communication.

I continued to call on these strengths many times in my position. As time went on in my role, nearly every year I had a new boss and change became my new norm. So at the start of each fiscal year, in conjunction with every boss change, I developed a new vision. I never recycled the old vision, but instead I would listen to what each new boss said and get in tune with that individual's own goals.

With this new understanding, I would incorporate the key points, create a new PowerPoint, and present my vision of how the department would work under the new leader's command. I'd get the new boss's buy in, and then I'd go back to the team and let them know what was decided. I'd communicate with them about whatever I'd learned the changes would be.

Maybe my message was that nothing would be changing except for our department name. Or maybe the only change was that we'd need to hire to fill a new position. Whatever changes I could inform them about, I'd do so. Part of my job as a manager was to translate the new boss's direction back over the fence to them and let them know what was going on to alleviate their fear of the unknown. Again, that's not managing a change, that's just knowing how to talk to people.

A Personal Example: Overcoming Resistance

Sometimes, of course, when communicating with people about changes that affect them I'd encounter resistance and, as discussed earlier, overcoming resistance is another common topic you'll find in change management courses. Yet I need to tell you that overcoming resistance has nothing to do with managing change. It's all about understanding human nature, knowing who's on your team, and responding to what their personal needs are; let me explain.

When I joined the company described above in a supervisory role, not only did I have new bosses to contend with, but new employees. One of my new charges had been with the company for 10 years on the day I walked in, working heads-down in the same department, happy as a clam. Yet I made a major mistake when I came in and rocked her boat without first getting to know her story.

What I saw on the outside and what this employee valued on the inside were two different things. What I saw was a high performer, one of our best in the group. I assumed the best way to reward her would be to promote her, and make her my second in command. Wrong answer.

Had I taken time to understand her story, I would have learned that she was the wife of a farmer—her hard-working husband also worked part-time as a postal worker. She had three kids who were her world, and she had left a great position at her last company to take her current position specifically to be closer to her family.

As it turned out, she had no desire to move up the ladder—she didn't want more responsibility, she wanted to keep a high level of flexibility to be able to attend family functions and be there for family needs.

Not knowing this, I proceeded down the wrong path with her for about three months, grooming her for a supervisory position. When she could take it no longer, she finally told me she had zero desire to be a manager, and that her stomach had been in knots ever since I'd suggested it.

In this case, once I became aware of my employee's resistance to change, I helped us both move beyond it by taking the time to understand her nature and personal needs. What she valued was time with her family. Taking time off to go see her son's concert or her daughter's school play energized her and made her more productive. It wasn't a promotion that motivated her, as I'd assumed.

All that was needed to solve the problem and make her resistance a non-issue was an understanding of human dynamics. I wasn't managing change when I solved this problem—I was learning about the personal life of a valued employee and responding to it accordingly, which every manager should do. Without understanding who your employees are as people, you'll never understand what motivates them as professionals.

A Personal Example: Sustaining Change

Looking back over my time at the medical device manufacturer, throughout all of the change that happened to me and to my employees, I never tried to manage the change itself. I never went to my boss's boss and said, "Can you please stop giving me new bosses?" because that wouldn't have worked. It also wouldn't have worked to say, "We want to stay the way we are. We don't want to move. We don't want to have to keep changing our vision."

Instead, I had to figure out first how to communicate, and second how to understand the human dynamics of my team. But there was something else I had to master as well, and that was how to sustain change over time—especially in an environment where change became the norm. And frankly, if you think about it, isn't that the case in most companies?

Once I saw the pattern of the yearly boss change, I got to the point where I would anticipate the next change. Whether or not the change would come again on the same schedule, I was ready for it and was never content to rest on my laurels with whatever program we had. I was always anticipating what the next boss might need and developed PowerPoints in anticipation of questions that I might be asked. I started imagining what question they would come up with next— maybe they'd ask about ROI this year or maybe about how a certain departmental system might be better run.

Quite simply, I didn't want to be caught off-guard by changes, so I prepared for them in advance. In this way, I helped my group to sustain the spirit of whatever change was happening at any given time, and prepare for what might happen next. Together we cultivated an environment that expected change and welcomed it.

From hereon in I'll be pulling out some "take-homes" from each piece of learning and here's the first one that seeks to encapsulate what we've discussed thus far:

> *Whether you initiate change or change happens to you, how you respond to that change is what really matters. That's the essence of true change leadership.*

If you can use the ideas above to help your management team and employees better respond to the changes they face, or even start to anticipate them, you'll have won half the battle—without calling in the "change management" trainers.

CHAPTER 4
WHY YOU CAN'T MANAGE TIME

Change isn't the only variable that can't be managed—another area that companies erroneously assume that they can manage is time. And like "change management," the concept of "time management" is also pushed hard in many leadership training courses.

Why can't time be managed? Because each of us gets the same 24 hours each day and that's non-negotiable. It can't be changed. No one can "manage" time to squeeze out a 25th hour miracle. Time marches on regardless of any employee's level of productivity, and no matter what individuals do or don't do during the day. It keeps moving forward at exactly the same rate no matter how hard someone might try to rein it in.

Yet employees can get better at managing which initiatives on their plate are priorities. They can link those initiatives to specific business goals that help drive their priorities. They can become better organized. They can also learn to simplify the processes they're using so that particular jobs become less time-consuming. Or, with the empowerment of their managers, they can take on fewer responsibilities, eliminating some duties that are currently taking up too much time.

Prioritization. Goals. Organization. Processes. Responsibilities. These things can be managed and, while they're each related to time, they aren't time itself. These areas are about managing tasks employees are doing, rather than trying to manage time itself. You might think about it as managing how employees *use* their time more efficiently. Therefore, instead of tackling the illusory goal of time management, employers should focus on helping staff manage their tasks.

Here are three reasons why it's important to understand the difference between managing time and managing tasks:

1. Time is money and it's a waste of both to invest in concepts that are inherently flawed.

2. Shifting your focus from the illusory concept of managing time to the realistic concept of managing tasks can be a transformative change in thinking that leads to improved ROI—instead of trying to wrap your head around an idea that isn't practical and can't be done, you move toward real options for circumventing corporate bottlenecks.

3. While time is a very general concept, tasks are specific. The fallacy behind time management is that every company can grab the same off-the-shelf solution to solve certain problems attributed to time management.

Let me elaborate on that last point. Since we all have the same number of hours in the day, we should be able to all use the same time training course, right? Wrong. When you realize that it's actually not time you're managing but tasks, then it becomes clear how every company, and every individual within that company, has unique tasks to manage.

Just as we saw with "change management," what helps one company become more efficient will not necessarily help yours. Only by understanding what *can* be managed in relation to tasks—and by analyzing the specific tasks that your people are trying to manage—can you help your employees and managers improve efficiencies.

TIME OUT

Before we go too much further into learning about the specifics of task management, I want to share a personal story to help illuminate the fallacy of time management.

I worked with an executive director of operations and maintenance for a large company (let's call him Ed). Ed had a team of about 10 employees with companywide responsibility and one day he came to me and said, "I just don't think my people are getting stuff done quickly enough. I'm going back to them, and the work is still sitting there."

So Ed asked me if I could provide a time management course to help solve these problems and, in turn, I asked him for an example of the types of problems he was having. He told me about a project that he'd given to a woman on his team, explaining that he'd left her an assignment and returned to her desk later in the day expecting that the work would be done, but found that she hadn't started it.

"So had you specified that you were expecting the work to be done that same day?" I asked and he shook his head. There was problem number one.

"And was this the only thing she had to do or did she have other tasks?"

"No this was an extra and she still had her day-to-day operations to contend with," he replied, now starting to see where I was going.

"And you didn't tell her that this particular project was more important than her day-to-day work?"

Again, now looking rather sheepish, he once more shook his head.

Now it was quite clear that before he spent money on a time management course, he had to tackle the following:

- Define for his employees what their day-to-day operations are;
- Define when those operations should be usurped by an incoming project;
- Discuss "one-off" project deadlines at the time each project is assigned.

I reminded Ed that each of the above items should be driven by the overall goals of his business, in order to set proper prioritization of day-to-day operations versus project work. In the same way as that oft quoted story of the NASA janitor who saw his job as helping put a man on the moon, he also had to ensure that each of his employees saw how their tasks linked to those organizational goals.

I assured Ed that if he tried these steps and still found that the assigned work was not getting done, then we'd talk about a time management course; a month later he assured me that he did not need one! After following the steps I'd outlined with each person on his team, he found that suddenly, his team was more productive and things were getting done!

When Ed shifted his focus from a nebulous sense of trying to control his employees' time to helping them better manage their tasks, he found there was no need to invest resources in a so-called time management course.

SELF-MANAGEMENT TRUMPS TIME MANAGEMENT

Here's another example: I've talked with many a work-group manager, organization leader, or company president who is convinced that productivity is being lost because employees are spending too much time around the water cooler (or on Facebook, personal calls, or whatever the individual case may be).

These leaders are certain that this is a time management issue, rationalizing that if they could eliminate the half hour spent at the water cooler, it would solve the problem and employees would be more productive—but there is a flaw in thinking here.

It's inherently wrong to believe that simply corralling people back to their desks and eliminate their group coffee breaks—or block Facebook from company computers or prohibit personal calls—the employees in question will automatically become more productive. It doesn't necessarily follow that just because you try to eliminate distractions from an employee's work day that he or she will then channel the new-found time into working smarter, and this is because the *biggest* time management myth assumes that work output is directly related to the amount of time someone has available to put into a task.

Maybe your employees will be so disgruntled by having their version of the "water cooler" removed that they'll disengage more from their work than before. Maybe the water cooler break actually recharged some employees to do their best work of the day immediately following it. I'd strongly suggest that such an action is going to make them feel much less engaged, so here are some different ideas.

Because of these "maybes": maybe it would pay for managers to do the opposite? Instead of pulling the plug on any activity seen as a potential "water cooler," take the completely opposite approach and take time to discover what constitutes a "water cooler" for each employee.

Research by Gallup and other organizations has clearly shown that engaged employees are more productive employees. Gallup estimates that in the U.S. workforce, the cost of actively disengaged employees results in more than $300 billion in lost productivity. Yet as you'll see in the following case study, providing employees with the flexibility to enjoy what helps recharge them can lead to better engagement, which corresponds with a proven ROI on key business metrics.

FIND THE WATER COOLER

I know what some of you may be thinking right now—you simply want your work to get done, and having warm and fuzzy, super-satisfied employees is not your priority as a business owner. But bear with me and let me prove that this concept ties directly to your employees' productivity levels and your company's bottom line. Here's a real-world example from the mega-retailer *Best Buy*.

Following an initiative to find out what each of their employees thinks of as a "water cooler" activity and doing something about it, the results were staggering: An average productivity increase of 35 percent was achieved along with a decrease in voluntary turnover of up to 90 percent. You all know the issue of the cost of staff recruitment—and we will discuss this in chapter 7—so think of the savings that greater level of organizational commitment provided.

Best Buy's strategy is called ROWE, which stands for Results Only Work Environment. First implemented in 2003 by Jody Thompson and Cali Ressler, ROWE means that the majority (80 percent) of their corporate staff have the freedom to structure their own work day, coming and going as they see fit, so long as they complete their work and fulfill their assigned responsibilities.

The beauty of this plan is that it actually *saves* management the trouble of determining the specifics of what constitutes each employee's water cooler activity. It just carves out space for these activities to occur, whatever they may be. Employees get to decide for themselves what to do and when. Under this system, they can ensure that their personal needs are met during the day, as long as the work gets done correctly and on time. It's liberating for employers and employees alike.

And *Best Buy* isn't the only high-profile company that's figured this out. Other large organizations that have implemented similar "officeless office" concepts include IBM, Sun Microsystems, and Google. Again, the proof is in the results: the *Seattle PI* reports that Google engineers have the opportunity to pursue their own interests for a full day each week—and more than half of Google's top innovations emerge during this "time out."

Do you see a theme here? Programs like ROWE revolve around *work*, not around *hours*. They're about *results*, not about the amount of *time* spent working. Such strategies have been proven to significantly increase productivity, yet they have nothing to do with time management—in fact, quite the opposite. They're about relinquishing the worry around trying to manage your staff's time, and instead relying on them, as responsible adults, to effectively manage their own tasks.

BECOMING A BETTER TASK MASTER

With that story in mind, let's take a closer look at those five key areas of task management—*prioritization, goals, organization, processes, and responsibilities*—and see how they can help your organization avoid wasting resources on time management training.

Even if you're a small to mid-sized business owner and not be ready to go the ROWE route just yet, you can still make a fundamental mental shift from time management to task management when you focus on these concepts.

#1 Prioritization

Since your employees can't change the amount of time that they have available to them each day, they must be able to determine what's most critical to do during their working hours. Learning how to prioritize is the cornerstone of effective task management, and the key to becoming more efficient.

Approaches such as the ROWE method empower employees to become masters of their own task management, but in order for them to do so with your business goals in mind, they must first hear from you about what's most important. Once you've communicated this, there's a certain element of trust involved in stepping out of the way so that they can get to work.

So instead of thinking about how to help employees manage their time better (which is a false concept), think about ways to encourage and empower them to best manage themselves in relation to time within their working hours. Some specific ideas on how to do this follow in the next four areas.

#2 Goals

To properly drive your prioritization initiatives, you need to first define your business goals and these are what your employees should be using as the backdrop for setting their own daily priorities. Without communicating very clearly about what you are trying to accomplish in each part of your business, your employees will not have the information that they need to make effective decisions around task management.

Remember our earlier examples of the NASA janitor and Ed, who learned to incorporate the overall goals of his business into determining project priorities for his team members? By doing so, he was able to better guide each person in properly prioritizing day-to-day operations versus incoming project work—resulting in greater productivity.

The ultimate vision is for you as the business owner or organization executive to "take your hands off the wheel" so that employees can manage their own tasks. But don't make the mistake of thinking you're off the hook when it comes to the initial steps of prioritization and goal setting. By taking the time to share overall business goals with each employee (or department head) and map out relevant priorities based on those goals, you'll be ensuring that employees are making *your* priorities *their* priorities.

The key to the effectiveness of this strategy starts and ends with you, and your ability to communicate your goals in a way that informs your staff's decision-making process. Otherwise, their priorities may not match yours, resulting in decreased productivity in the areas that mean the most to your business. But get this right, and especially as a business owner, and you'll be much closer to thinking personally about growth and working "on" your business and not "in" your business.

#3 Organization

When you examine the content of most time management courses, you'll see that they're actually peddling improved organizational skills. At the end of the day, it's great to be organized, and it helps to be disciplined, but don't call that time management.

I once was invited to a course that billed itself as "time management," relying on gimmicks such as a 9:09 published start time rather than 9:00. This training all but guaranteed if you followed their strategies, you'd regain an hour of lost time each day.

But outside of the odd start time, time-related information was conspicuous by its absence in the course itself, which was clearly more about how to be better organized. Like many time management classes, it hinged on principles originally popularized by productivity expert Stephen R. Covey about the best way to organize one's day.

For example, one of Covey's methods recommends categorizing tasks into four quadrants of important/urgent, important/not urgent, not important/urgent, and not important/not urgent—and prioritizing on the basis of those quadrants. If you guessed that the top priority tasks that must be done first are those in the first quadrant, you're right, but it wasn't difficult was it?!

Part of being organized is having the discipline to actually tackle the critical and important/urgent tasks first, rather than getting sucked into time wasters. It's human nature to want to begin by crossing the easy tasks off of our list rather than starting the day by rolling up our sleeves and digging into a major job that will move us further toward our goals.

When it comes to being productive, it takes more than just being organized and knowing what needs to be done first versus second and third. It takes the self-management to actually do it. This is where smart hiring comes in. If the person you hire for the job lacks the discipline to stay organized after you've explained your business goals, and their priorities around those goals, then knowing about the quadrants can't help them—and certainly no time management course can.

#4 Processes

Another way that employees can become task masters rather than clock watchers is by simplifying work-related processes to make jobs less time-consuming. I worked with a mid-sized label and package printing company that was worried about their team's level of productivity.

We did begin by looking at how people were spending their time, but we didn't stop there. In order to gain a solid understanding about what was hampering productivity, I helped the management team map out their actual sales process, from the time an order was taken to the time an invoice was sent out. We discovered there was a wide level of fluctuation in how long this process took to complete, which ranged anywhere from two weeks to two months.

In cases where the process stretched toward two months, employees lost efficiency by having to reinvent the wheel. Often staff would have to mentally repeat parts of the initial sales process by reviewing notes and getting back up to speed on something that was initiated weeks or months ago.

Instead of continuing on with this level of fluctuation, we stopped the process and went back to square one. We identified better ways for specific departments to contribute at different junctures to move the whole process forward more quickly. We found ways to eliminate bottlenecks and implement workarounds for parts of the process that were holding up entire orders.

Until we went through the exercise of mapping out the process from start to finish, no one knew where the problem areas were, or how to fix them. Time was being wasted through an inefficient process, but a time management course wouldn't have helped this company. Even organizing and prioritizing by quadrants wouldn't have helped.

What helped was going back and seeing what went wrong, and figuring out how to prevent it from happening again. What made the difference was changing the company's process, so teams could work more efficiently and be more productive.

#5 Responsibilities

Once again, you can't manage time, but just as you can help guide employees to better manage their own priorities, goals, organizational skills, and processes, you can also help regulate their responsibilities. In fact, this is a crucial part of effective leadership. In most cases, employees don't design their own responsibilities, but depend on the management team to provide clear direction in this area.

Responsibilities are intricately linked to employee effectiveness. If people have too much to do in the amount of time that they have to do it in, then they will be less productive than they could be. Tailoring responsibilities is one of the best ways that managers can help their teams reach business goals.

For managers, this process ideally begins before hiring a team. Creating clear and realistic job descriptions that accurately reflect each position's true responsibilities is the first step in steering your group toward maximum effectiveness.

Avoid the trap of assigning too many responsibilities to any individual team member, as this strategy will likely backfire. By the same token, you don't want to underutilize staff by failing to provide enough stretch opportunities to keep them motivated *and engaged.* Providing employees with an appropriate level of responsibility encourages greater productivity, and creates a win-win for you and your employees.

Here's the next take-home:

> *While time management is a myth, task management isn't.*

By providing the leadership needed to guide your teams toward better self-management through the five key areas of task management (prioritization, goals, organization, processes, and responsibilities), you can improve employee efficiency, company productivity and that all-important bottom line.

CHAPTER 5
WHY YOU CAN'T MANAGE STRESS

We've clarified why change and time can't be managed. But what about stress?

As a small business owner, you may be tempted to follow the lead set by many larger companies that have embraced the idea of trying to solve staff challenges and improve business outcomes through stress management training. This would be a big mistake, because you can't manage stress any more than you can manage changes that have already been decided, or manage the number of hours you get per day.

STRESSED OVER STRESS MANAGEMENT

The corporate world has bought in big-time to the myth that workplace stress can be managed. In fact, nearly half of all large companies in the United States provide stress management training for their employees, according to the National Institute for Occupational Safety and Health

(NIOSH), and there's a good reason why. Company leadership is seeking solutions to stress in the workplace because, according to the NIOSH research, organizations that promote healthy policies for low-stress work environments are associated with higher levels of productivity.

NIOSH also notes that stress on the job is linked with several problems that can affect productivity, such as employees coming late to work more often, missing more days of work, and considering quitting their jobs. According to the Bureau of Labor Statistics (BLS), workers who take time off due to stress-related complaints are out of the office for four weeks on average.

In the case of small to mid-sized businesses, issues like this can be even more damaging. When retention starts to be affected, having to rehire and retrain employees can have a big impact on cost and in lost time, yet there's a problem here in turning to stress management training for solutions.

According to author and workplace expert Alexander Kjerulf, a recent study revealed that people attending stress management training actually reported feeling *greater* stress than those who didn't attend. Kjerulf's read on these findings is that most classes dubbed "stress management" focus on the experience of stress itself, which magnifies stress in people's minds rather than reducing it.

Dwelling on stress-related topics such as, "Do I have stress symptoms?" and "How can I tell if I'm too stressed?"—which are commonly included in stress management courses—can certainly create more stress and anxiety.

The American Psychological Association (APA) reports that "no universally effective stress reduction techniques exist." Therefore, the organization concludes that what we've discussed about change and time is also true for stress: that the most popular techniques are not the best ones.

Says the APA: "We are all different, our lives are different, our situations are different, and our reactions are different. Only a comprehensive program tailored to the individual works." They took the words right out of my mouth.

THERE ARE DIFFERENT LEVELS OF STRESS

Stressors are not all created equal, although it may feel like it sometimes—as Lee Iacocca has said, "stress is the confusion created when one's mind overrides the body's basic desire to choke the living daylights out of some jerk who desperately deserves it!"

But in reality, there is a continuum of possible reactions to stressors that runs from minor annoyance to "code blue" feelings of stress that can seriously affect the health of the person who is experiencing it (not to mention the recipient of the stressful blast).

To give you a better idea of what I'm talking about, I think of stress—and reactions to it—as falling under the following four levels:

Level 1

This first level comprises "everyday stress" like traffic jams, broken appliances, and being late to a meeting. Though these stressors are a nuisance, most people see everyday stress as a minor annoyance rather than a serious problem.

We generally retain conscious awareness of our actions and reactions to stress at this level, which allows us to use our strengths to move through everyday stress relatively smoothly under normal circumstances.

Level 2

This is what I call "performance stress" and can come into effect when employees are under a deadline that they feel is too short. This can cause an "under the gun" type of pressure, leading to a more elevated feeling of stress than everyday stressors.

General responses to Level 2 stress may include either trying to get out of the assignment, or rising to the occasion. In the case of the latter, employees may come out the other side doing something amazing by pushing their comfort zone, but they are probably an exception.

Though people may be less conscious of their actions because of the intense level of focus demanded by performance stress, these situations can lead people to emphasize their strengths, producing "above and beyond" performance. But in a more common scenario, this level of stress can lead to greatly heightened anxiety in trying to perform in ways beyond which people feel capable.

Level 3

The third level feels something like "Argh!" and I refer to this as "losing control stress." Here, employees may feel that the stress is so upsetting that they must take action to regain composure and become calmer.

Although the action taken may be a healthy behavior such as a good workout in the gym, typically the action is a more destructive behavior. This might include smoking, overeating, compulsive if not dangerous exercise, drinking too much alcohol, or taking drugs. In the latter instances, the urge to decompress can lead to unhealthy behaviors that can become life-threatening if taken to extreme.

Another problem with this level of stress is that when people experience it they are usually so upset that they become self-absorbed, lacking awareness of the effects of their actions.

Level 4

The only thing worse than "losing control" is "flip out stress." At this point, people experiencing stress move beyond feeling that taking a concrete action would help with coping. Instead, they experience a brief feeling of, "That's enough—I can't take it any longer!" and either explode or shut down. When you say, "He's finally snapped," you're talking about "flip out" stress.

Often this extreme level of stress expresses itself in causing people to act totally out of character. For an introvert, this might mean an outburst of energy rather than staying calmly behind the scenes, perhaps slamming a pen on a table or storming out of the room. Extraverts under level 4 stress might suddenly retreat to be on their own for a while.

In both cases, the flip out stage represents coming to the end of your rope in terms of resources to try to deal with stress. Unfortunately, this level also exposes our weaknesses in an immature form—the classic "bad hair day."

DIFFERENT PEOPLE EXPERIENCE STRESS DIFFERENTLY

Because of this wide range of possible reactions to perceived stressors, it would be quite difficult to design a class that successfully addresses each one, and the same goes with the fact that people express their stress differently.

Traditional stress management training approaches stress as a uniform sensation, suggesting that it can be wrangled into compliance. They don't treat it as a range of experiences that people may need to find different ways to handle, depending on the level of how they experience particular stressors.

Just as the causes of stress can vary, then so too can the models for handling it. Employees each have a unique perspective that forms their perception, which becomes their version of reality. What one of your employees finds stressful, another may find invigorating. For example, one employee's level 3 office stressor might include giving presentations to the group, while another employee may thrive on being in the spotlight. Still another may only feel level 1 stress from this same situation.

In addition to variation of stressors among employees, the management team likely has different stressors than their direct reports—as well as from each other. Some managers may get stressed when they have to write reports, while others may excel at written reports. And you as the CEO may not share the same stressors with either your management team or your employees—or at least not all of them.

Therefore, there's no "catch-all" strategy that can help an entire work group effectively manage stress. If everyone's stressors are different, then one size of training can't fit all.

SOME PEOPLE MAY BE THE CAUSE OF THEIR OWN STRESS

The point above gets at the fact that stress is a largely individualized experience. The perception of stress is stored in our subconscious, and how we perceive ourselves and view the world varies among people. It follows then that some people, including your employees, may be exacerbating their experience of it.

How can employees make their own stress worse? The way that they think about things plays a major role in how they feel about them. Andrew Bernstein, author of *The Myth of Stress*, notes that stress doesn't result from what's actually happening in your life—it comes from how you *think* about what's happening.

Says Bernstein: "Popular 'stress management' tools relieve the *effects* of stress, but not the *cause,* so the stress returns again and again. A more effective long-term approach involves learning to think differently about challenging situations, so the stress is no longer produced."

If your employees perceive certain issues in the workplace as stressful—for example, fearing upcoming change in the organization, or feeling like they lack the time to get their job done because they are doing a poor job at task management—then their thoughts may be influencing their stress level at work. It's counterproductive to waste time and money trying to help employees deal with the effects of stress without modifying the cause, which in some cases comes from the employees themselves.

MANY STRESSORS ARE OUT OF YOUR CONTROL

There are some cases where employees actually may be able to exert some control over the stressors that they face. For example, staff may be able to influence their workload by telling their supervisor that they have too much on their plate to take on a new project. However, they can't control how their supervisor will respond to their request and if stress is self-initiated due to fears, concerns, or worries, people then have to work on controlling how they perceive certain situations.

In many instances, it's impossible for people to manage the cause of their stress because many stressors are not under their control. Stress is more often something that "just happens" to people for various reasons that we have no influence over whatsoever. Examples of this, both inside and out of the office, are endless, but to name a few that no one can control:

- Traffic they hit on the way to work;
- If it rains when they go on vacation;
- Whether their supervisor needs them to work overtime, causing them to miss their child's piano recital.

Each of these situations is out of your employees' control—as are so many other possible scenarios. All that's in their control is to handle how they respond.

BENEFICIAL EFFECTS OF "TREATMENT" ON STRESS-RELATED SYMPTOMS DON'T LAST LONG

According to NIOSH, stress management programs have a major disadvantage: Even in cases where such programs succeed in alleviating some stress symptoms, those benefits tend to be short-lived. This is because the goal of stress management is almost always to manage the results of stress, not the root causes of it. They focus on fixing the worker, but ignore the environment that surrounds the worker.

For example, in the wake of stress management training, employees may try implementing strategies designed to improve certain symptoms of stress, such as anxiety or forgetfulness. And they may experience a reduction in symptoms initially.

But if the source of the stressors that are causing the symptoms of anxiety and forgetfulness are not identified and effectively managed, the benefits of treating the symptoms will only last as long as the next stressful episode—at which point the same strategies would need to be repeated all over again.

THE REAL ANSWERS

Clearly, stress management is not the answer. There is a growing chorus from workplace experts, including the federal agency charged with occupational safety and health, pointing out the flaws in stress management training.

That doesn't mean, however, that there are no viable solutions to the productivity challenges of stress in the workplace. It just means you have to think beyond the quick-fix promise of stress management courses to strategies that will bring about real and lasting change in your business or organization.

Employees can learn how to cope better with stressors and more effectively handle their response to stress, but they must have support from management. What your leaders need to recognize is that they can play a crucial role in discovering individual differences in stressors between employees in order to create a work environment with lower stress and higher productivity.

Upon discovering the limitations of stress management programs, many forward-thinking companies are embracing the following ideas:

Promote a Healthy Workplace, don't Manage a Stressful One

What you focus on expands. As discussed earlier, focusing on the problem of stress doesn't necessarily lead to solutions, and, as Kjerulf noted, research shows that focusing on stress may cause people to feel more stressed than ever.

However, research suggests a better strategy is promoting policies that benefit worker wellness—an anti-stress approach, if you will. Rather than putting stress front and center, this approach prioritizes creating a healthy, low-stress workplace.

What creates for a low-stress workplace? NIOSH studies have identified the following characteristics of healthy organizations, which are defined as having low rates of employee injury, illness, and disability while remaining competitive in the marketplace:

- Providing opportunities for career development;
- Recognizing employees for their work performance;
- Valuing individuals through organizational culture;
- Ensuring management actions reflect organizational values.

Companies that prioritize maintaining a healthy work environment have less stress to manage in their workforce, and accompanying higher levels of productivity.

Think Environment Management, Not Stress Management

When you shift the focus from "fixing stress" to "fixing the workplace problems that cause stress," you're moving in the right direction. As we saw when exploring the fallacies of change and time management, solving workplace challenges in any arena can only be effectively done on a case-by-case basis.

The stress-related challenges in your workplace aren't the same as in another company, so taking a generic stress management approach is foolish. Trying to manage the outcomes of stress without modifying the causes of those outcomes is equally so.

To circumvent the limitations of stress management programs, NIOSH suggests implementing organizational change specifically by bringing in an outside facilitator. The value of turning to third parties is that they can recommend objective ways to improve your company's *specific* challenges in relation to employee stress. In fact, the website for the Center for Disease Control—CDC, of which NIOSH is an arm—states that this approach is "the most direct way to reduce stress at work."

Managing the work environment may sound like a tall order, especially when compared with the quick-fix promise of a 30-minute lunch and learn. The difference is that the former strategy can bring about the long-term improvements needed to prevent dents in your company's productivity, while the latter can never do so on its own.

As a business owner or company executive you may cringe at the thought of needing to make shifts in employee work routines, production schedules, or even departmental or organizational structure to bring about the desired results. Yet the reason that environment management can succeed where stress management fails is that, once again, like change leadership and task management, it's based on customized solutions.

Environment management is about identifying stressful aspects of work that your staff might be experiencing, and designing strategies to reduce or remove these stressors. In other words, it's about dealing directly with the root causes of stress at work, which could be anything from workload to conflicting expectations to differences in communication styles. Your solutions to manage the work environment will depend completely on the specific stressors identified, and I'll now turn to how you identify these employee-specific stressors.

Think Local, Not Global

In many cases in business, global is good. The theory behind global applications is that a single solution will indeed fit every circumstance, and it's great when these work because you only have to worry about one rollout for everyone—hence the temptation to use prepackaged training solutions.

Wouldn't life be grand, and so much simpler, if we could simply take a global approach to stress management as well? Unfortunately, you now see that it just doesn't work effectively that way. As NIOSH states on the CDC website:

> *"No standardized approaches or simple 'how to' manuals exist for developing a stress prevention program. Program design and appropriate solutions will be influenced by several factors—the size and complexity of the organization, available resources, and especially the unique types of stress problems faced by the organization."*

So instead of going global, I encourage you to think more "locally" as you work to identify specific stressors that might be negatively affecting you employees, and thus company productivity.

One very concrete way to put this idea into practice is to think of your employees "locally" rather than globally as well. What I mean by this is that rather than thinking of your employees as a uniform group who all respond the same way to different workplace variables, you should see them as individuals who are each affected differently by potential stressors.

I described earlier how different people experience stress differently—but how can you as a business owner or company executive use this fact to help improve each employee's stress level, and thus productivity? One way is to use a tool like *Insights Discovery*®, an assessment application designed to capture and call out individual preferences, as well as the differences between people and what they're likely to perceive as stressful.

Managers can use this feedback to better understand what different employees might find stressful, and also to understand why employees might perceive situations differently from one another. With this information in hand, managers and employees alike can play a role in making specific changes to the work environment as needed. We'll learn a little more about specific ways that you might use *Insights* in your organization in the following sections.

Think Managing Reactions, Not Managing Stress

While no one can control all of the stressors that they face, everyone can control how they interpret—and thus react to—those stressors. It's about coping with stress rather than managing stress and this is a two-part process. In order to help employees effectively address stress, company leaders first need to determine what is causing individual employees, or certain departments or parts of the company, to feel upset or worried.

There are many ways to approach gathering this information, including employee/departmental surveys and utilizing information from performance reviews. But the most straightforward method involves simply communicating with employees to get to the bottom of their true experience. Many businesses that I've worked with have found *Insights Discovery*® to be particularly helpful in this regard.

By having employees answer a series of online questions about their working style, preferences, and behaviors; this tool provides work groups with extensive "profile" information that contains valuable clues as to individual communication styles that can be beneficial, and how different people are likely to respond to various workplace situations.

After determining the types of scenarios that are likely to cause stress for each team member, managers can move on to the second part of the process. This involves assessing these findings and reinforcing learning to help employees make behavior changes in the areas identified as stress-producing. In other words, managers can help their teams cope with stress better and react to stressful solutions more effectively. The strategies that follow expand on some ideas about how to do this.

Think Offer a Framework, Not Impose a Training

Since there is no universal prescription for preventing stress at work, the best thing you can do for your staff is offer a general framework to help them handle it. The framework that I like to use when working with small to mid-sized businesses, or perhaps divisions of larger ones, is called ARC, which stands for "**A**wareness and acknowledgement," "**R**espond accordingly," and "**C**ool down and recharge."

ARC BEFORE YOU SPARK!

This is a great way to remind employees of the role that this framework can play and I'll walk you through some of the basics.

Awareness and Acknowledgement

This first step of the framework is to help employees learn to identify their unique stressors. Awareness can be empowering, whereas things that we are unaware of can more easily gain control over us. So this step is really all about helping employees know themselves better, Socrates style, and understand what they want and don't want.

This is another area where *Insights Discovery*® can offer a solid jumpstart, since it allows individuals to gain information about themselves that they can use to recognize their own causes of stress. Work groups can share this information with each other to build awareness about what situations cause stress for themselves and others, as well as acknowledge these differences in various team members to promote better working harmony.

For example, the *Insights* model results essentially in self-identification as one of four main "color energies": cool blue, earth green, sunshine yellow or fiery red. Here are the differences between what tends to "stress out" each color energy preference:

- **Cool Blue:** lack of information, structure, or logic; poor quality work; time wasted; task rushed;
- **Earth Green:** unfair or impersonal treatment; violation of core values; interruptions; time pressures;
- **Sunshine Yellow:** restriction or lack of flexibility; lack of interaction; environment that is too serious with no room for fun; personal rejection;
- **Fiery Red:** lack of focus; indecisiveness; lack of control.

When employees have awareness of what types of issues are likely to bring on stressful feelings in themselves and others, they can use it to manage their own reactions to stress, as well as to avoid triggering stressful feelings in others.

Additionally, work groups can learn to identify certain stress signals for each color type. By having awareness of these signals—which are expressed when people experience their unique stressors—work teams will have a much better chance of stress reaction control through recognition and acknowledgement of individual differences:

- **Cool Blue:** becomes aloof, withdrawn and resentful; questioning and deliberate; nitpicking;
- **Earth Green:** becomes silent, withdrawn or hurt; judgmental; impersonal; resistant and stubborn; overly cautious;
- **Sunshine Yellow:** becomes over-responsive; opinionated; argumentative;
- **Fiery Red:** becomes aggressive; impatient; irritable; demanding.

Respond Accordingly

Once your work teams have a basic awareness of what causes stress and can recognize signs of trouble, they need to know how to respond appropriately. My grandmother would often cite the Serenity Prayer to me during times of stress and I often use it in my work:

God, grant me the serenity to accept the things I cannot change,
Courage to change the things I can,
And wisdom to know the difference.

Grandma was right, because knowing the difference between what you can change—and what you can't—lies behind every appropriate response. So here's what I recommend that you share with your teams:

1. As soon as you become aware of stressful feelings, take time to identify the stressor. Think about why this situation is upsetting you out. People crave balance between three aspects of themselves: their thoughts, actions, and emotions. When those aspects of your life are in balance, you have personal synergy. But the more out of whack those three things get, the more stress you'll experience. So figure out what it is about any given workplace situation that causes your personal synergy to be compromised.

2. Recognize that you always have a choice about how to react—even if that choice is to do nothing at the moment. It can also help to get more comfortable with the word "no" to help set your boundaries and avoid taking on more than you can reasonably handle.

3. Remember that you are not alone in facing workplace stress. Be willing to ask for help from your manager and coworkers, and accept assistance to help you move past crisis points.

Cool Down and Recharge

Part of every appropriate response should involve a recovery period. I recommend working with your management team to put a system in place for stress recovery. Empower your employees to use a cool-down period after stressful situations.

Your system might involve encouraging staff to take a time out, putting some distance between themselves and the fray. This may mean a walk around the block, an early lunch break, or just some time in a quiet conference room to take a few deep breaths before pushing on.

On a longer-term scale, encourage your teams to find what works for each individual for ongoing self-care. On a basic level, employees should be informed that they can reduce their feelings of stress dramatically simply by practicing healthy habits. Without enough sleep, exercise, and a proper diet, no one can function at their best, and stress responses can be exaggerated or inappropriate.

Some team members may benefit from spending more of their leisure time with family and friends, while others might need less interaction and more quiet time during their off-hours to take care of their mental health. Promote a work environment that values and honors these differences.

Here's the take-home:

> *Stress can't be managed but reactions to stress—as well as stressful environments—can be and should be. By offering employees a framework to handle stress that begins with their own awareness, you can promote a low-stress workplace linked with greater productivity.*

You have tools at your disposal to help in these areas. Use them to develop customized stress solutions for your employees, and your company will experience greater retention and better bottom-line performance.

PART II

The Consequences of Taking the Wrong Approach to Development

CHAPTER 6

WHY YOU CAN'T MANAGE <INSERT TOPIC HERE>

By this stage in the book, it should be clear that something has indeed gone wrong with many standard leadership development approaches. When you try to manage the unmanageable, the content of your program almost doesn't matter—the point is, you're funneling your time and resources into things that can't be fixed.

To that point, I'd like to add that although we've focused specifically on the misguided principle of "managing" change, stress, and time, what's gone wrong with developing leaders really goes far beyond these three areas. In fact, I'd even argue that you can name a different topic and I will tell you why it can't be managed or manipulated without a full understanding of the issues beneath the surface. Don't believe me? Let's try it.

Communication is another area that is often offered up for easy training solutions. But how can you coach a team in effective communication without knowing what the underlying issues are that your particular team finds problematic when it comes to communicating with one another? Simply teaching them generic interpersonal techniques, such as active listening or assertive communication, will fall on deaf ears—if you'll excuse the pun—if these aren't the specific tools that your team needs.

Your team members may know how to communicate just fine when it comes to the latest techniques. Yet when their various styles are cobbled together (which is in essence the nature of teamwork), the result may be not unlike the childhood game "Telephone," where the person at the end of the chain of whispered messages ends up with a garbled and completely different version of the original missive.

This is because what are often behind communication challenges are different styles of communicators. We've already discussed how assessment applications like *Insights Discovery*® can help identify individual preferences and differences in perceived stressors among team members, and such assessments can also help pinpoint differences in communication styles, and preferred ways of giving and receiving information. Having this information at the outset can help nip many potential communication problems in the bud much more effectively than training employees in general communication skills.

Let's try another example: workplace conflict. How many companies try to deal with conflict or improve office politics through traditional training methods? Can't we simply teach employees conflict-resolution techniques and get back to business? Unfortunately, it rarely works that way. What good are general techniques when there are so many variables to the types of conflict situations that employees may encounter?

Solutions must be tailored to specific problems when it comes to conflict resolution and, as with communication, it often comes down to individual style. Assessment tools can help identify patterns in how different people prefer to respond to conflict, as well as what styles they find overly confrontational in others. When employers and employees are aware of these nuances among their team members, they can avoid or address conflict in a meaningful way, based on what's most relevant to their teams.

Here's another one: employee satisfaction. Some training programs are targeted at improving retention by trying to improve employee satisfaction throughout a company. Do you see anything wrong with this picture? What makes John a more satisfied employee will not necessarily help you to retain Lisa. In fact, companywide initiatives that you implement as part of a general retention strategy may increase John's satisfaction while making Lisa less satisfied. Research has shown that this can happen especially if they are from different generations.

As can currently happen, when we have multiple generations of employees working shoulder to shoulder in the workplace—all at different ages and stages of their careers—there is simply no way that generic retention-based satisfaction programs can work. For example, each generation has different predilections toward how they view time and flexibility at work, and how much they value work-life balance. Therefore, any corporate strategies in these arenas should be designed with such distinctions in mind, rather than rolled out uniformly, in order to improve chances of actually increasing employee satisfaction.

OLD NOTIONS = SAME OLD SOLUTIONS

I'm sure you get the picture. What's gone wrong has gone wrong *across the board* when it comes to leadership development. But why is this so? Why are companies failing so completely in their attempted development initiatives? I believe that a major reason is that companies are trying to address their current problems—and anticipate future ones—by doing what they've always done instead of taking more innovative approaches.

The past was about off-the-shelf solutions and traditional training, from a time when some of these solutions may have had a better chance of working. This was before current technologies made our workplace so global and so 24-7, and today's concepts and diverse needs didn't exist to the same extent among leadership or employees.

A few decades ago, we didn't have those distinct generations trying to collaborate in the office. Workers had more in common before the advent of social media, smartphones, and the multitude of other ways that new technologies have encroached upon the workplace, for better or for worse. Though we've always been individuals at work, we weren't dealing with the same ballgame (or even universe) in terms of the level of change, pressure of time, degree of stress, and number of possible communication alternatives available to employees. In this relatively less complex environment, yesterday's training was born.

What wasn't a problem yesterday has become a big one today. Many companies are still basing their training efforts on archaic notions that were forged when the business world was a completely different place. What's gone wrong is that many companies have failed to adjust their employee and leadership development initiatives to keep up with the times, and sticking with the old means using a flawed premise when viewed through a more current lens.

To make this point clearer, we can compare what's happening in leadership development with what's happening in education. Creativity expert Ken Robinson has pointed out that while educational paradigms have changed dramatically over time having originated in the 18th and 19th centuries, our education system hasn't kept pace in the way that we're educating our children.

Robinson advocates a radical rethink of our approach to education in order to better cultivate creativity and incorporate the many different types of learning that we're aware of today. By clinging to old rules in how we teach our kids—such as going by the former assumption that working hard and getting a degree guarantees a good job—we jeopardize not only our children's future, but society's. Says Robertson, "The problem is that the current system of education was designed, conceived and structured for a different age."

Failing to adapt our school system to today's realities leads to a number of troubling trends, from a rise in dropout rates and attention-deficit disorders among students to a dwindling participation in the arts. These are the costs and consequences in the field of education of applying yesterday's models to today's students. As you'll discover in the coming chapters, there are comparable costs in the business world of using outdated leadership development for today's workers.

COSTS AND CONSEQUENCES

Perhaps as you've been reading, you've wondered, "What difference does it make that "managing" is a misnomer when it comes to leadership development? What's the worst that can happen by using tools and training that aren't as effective as they could be? At least my people are staying engaged by learning *something*...aren't they?"

The answer to those questions, I'm afraid, is no and your employees aren't staying engaged by using this approach. In fact, as we saw in Part I of the book, a major consequence of using leadership development that doesn't work is employee disengagement. In case you think that disengagement is not your company's biggest problem, think again.

Disengagement results in far more than simply having unhappy employees to deal with—and as we've discussed, satisfaction does not necessarily translate into engagement anyway. Disengaged employees lead to a number of challenges and these are not just for the affected individuals, but also for the organization as a whole.

A number of negative business outcomes can emerge from disengagement, which range from the emotional costs of low morale and high turnover, to the productivity costs that result from less committed employees. Engaged employees are much more focused on quality and growth, and they also stay with organizations longer. They produce more while creating better emotional engagement with customers, thus making more money for their company.

Like it or not, Gallup research shows that employee engagement is a leading indicator of an organization's overall performance outcomes, including financial performance. In other words, as we're about to explore in detail, the costs of inadequate training cannot be underestimated.

CHAPTER 7

EMOTIONAL COSTS: THE CANARY IN THE COAL MINE

"Employee engagement = Heightened emotional and intellectual connection that an employee has for his/her job, organization, manager or co-workers that, in turn, influences him/her to apply additional discretionary effort to his/her work."

–The Conference Board

"Researchers have explored the employee engagement construct in depth, finding that it consists of cognitive, emotional, and behavioral components…engaged employees have intellectual and emotional commitments to their work, thereby creating deeper attachments to their jobs and organizations and leading to heightened performance."

–Deloitte Consulting, LLP

"Over the past several decades, business and psychological researchers—including Gallup—have identified a strong relationship between employees' workplace engagement and their respective company's overall performance."

–Gallup, Inc.

If you've been wondering if your company's approach to training falls into the category of "what's gone wrong," there are some clues you can use to find out. Look around you. Do your teams—from the bottom up—display poor teamwork? Do you notice employees expressing anger, fear, depression, or fatigue either directly or indirectly? Have you seen managers and employees alike showing signs of stress or apathy? Is there an overall sense of low morale permeating your group? Are people calling out sick a lot? If so, there's a good chance that you're dealing with a disengaged workforce.

If this is the case, you're not alone. Recent Gallup research revealed that 71 percent of workers are either "not engaged" in their work, or "actively disengaged" from it. This figure remained fairly stable throughout all four quarters of 2011, according to Gallup's Employee Engagement Index. According to other Gallup studies on workplace engagement trends, the percentage hasn't changed much over the past decade.

Employee engagement—as you can see from both The Conference Board and Deloitte quotes heading this chapter—is intimately involved with emotional connection. And as Gallup's research suggests, many studies have shown that this connection (or lack of it) is linked with company performance and business outcomes.

It's also linked with development opportunities, or lack thereof. Leigh Branham, author of *The 7 Hidden Reasons Employees Leave: How to Recognize the Subtle Signs and Act Before It's Too Late*, identified "too few growth and advancement opportunities" as one of the reasons that employees fly the coop. Branham sites studies that show that while 85 percent of employees value career growth and development as a key reward, less than half say their companies are providing it adequately.

Part of effective development involves coaching and feedback, yet more than 60 percent of employees—particularly younger ones—say that they get too little feedback from their managers, making this another reason why they leave. Failure to develop staff from the ground up means that pipelines to leadership positions aren't filled with qualified candidates, leaving many companies vulnerable to management problems and high turnover. And, as already discussed, high turnover is expensive.

ADDING IT UP

Whatever the reason behind disengagement, the opening quotes above take a more troubling turn for business owners and executives when you do the reverse math. Gallup's statistics reveal that out of the entire U.S. workforce, only a third of employees show the type of emotional connection to their workplace that can lead to greater productivity. For employers and business owners, this means that there is a good chance that the vast majority of your company's talent is either untapped, left on the table, or about to walk out the door.

None of these scenarios are good, and all will cost your company time and money. In the worst-case latter scenario, talent that walks can be extremely pricey. A study by the Society for Human Resource Management (SHRM) estimated that the cost to replace a single eight-bucks-an-hour employee is $3,500. That's because every part of the hiring process must be considered and tallied, from recruiting to interviewing to training, and not to mention the reduction in productivity caused by ramp-up time for new employees.

The numbers escalate, of course, the higher the level of employee. A typical ballpark of the cost of losing entry-level employees amounts to 30 to 50 percent of their annual salary. But the number shoots up to 150 percent of salary for mid-level employees, and up to the 400 percent for high-level, specialized employees. To put a dollar figure to it, the cost to replace just one supervisor whose average annual pay is $40,000 would be $50,000. If your company loses five supervisors at this level per year, you'd be down $250,000 in bottom-line cost. And if your supervisors make more than $40,000 . . . well, you do the math.

We'll dig deeper into the full ramifications of the financial fallout caused by disengagement in Chapter 8. But lest you think that your troubles are confined to specific employees and that your positive "one third" can make up for the attitude shortfall of the rest, keep in mind that negativity can be contagious. The influence of even a few actively disengaged employees can often cause operational and performance issues to spread to other co-workers. When it comes to disengagement, no matter how small the number of those initially affected, it's best to nip it in the bud before it blooms.

CATCHING THE EARLY WARNING SIGNS

As we learned back in Chapter 1, employee disengagement serves as a clear harbinger that your leadership development efforts are failing. Your leaders aren't inspiring the type of effective engagement that drives a company's overall productivity, performance, and growth. Emotional costs—revealed through the types of clues mentioned at the start of this chapter—are often only the first layer indicating corporate dysfunction.

You may be tempted, as a CEO or entrepreneur, to turn a blind eye to the emotional costs of disengagement, preferring to set your sights squarely on the bottom line. Yet ignoring this first level of disengagement is a false economy. While emotional costs are problematic in themselves and can wreak havoc in the workplace, it's equally important to recognize that a lack of commitment in your employees means that you're likely a banana peel away from the even larger challenges of retention problems and high turnover.

Emotional costs are not "soft" costs. They're the canary in the coal mine that means your company's bottom line may soon be in jeopardy. As a business owner or company leader, it's your job to heed the canary by addressing any and all signs of emotional "check-out" in your workforce before it's too late. If you write this step off as being too warm and fuzzy, reread the previous paragraph. Just as emotional costs are not soft costs, neither are emotional skills soft skills.

To that end, one of the most powerful questions that leaders can ask themselves is, "Do I have an action plan to become a more emotionally aware leader?" Becoming more emotionally aware requires a dual-faceted approach: being "tuned in" to your employees' level of engagement, as well as being the type of leader who is not afraid to appropriately express your own emotions to better connect with your employees.

EMOTIONAL AWARENESS ACTION PLAN

To avoid being a leader who negatively impacts the emotional awareness of your management team, which could eventually hurt your whole company, you need to prepare against such an eventuality. Consider using the following two-pronged approach—one prong for your employees, and one prong for you—as a guide.

Tuning In to Them

We launched this chapter with some warning signs that you may soon have (or already have) "sick canaries" in your midst. The only way to nurse those birds back to health, and thus keep the coal mine functioning and productive, is to be aware of their malaise and treat it. As the former CEO of PepsiCo Steve Reinemund once said, "If people don't grow, the company doesn't grow."

If you're the kind of leader who doesn't want to focus on employees at the emotional level—figuring as long as the work's getting done today, it's all good—you may be in for a rude awakening next quarter or next year. That awakening may come in the form of excessive turnover, unexpected costs of replacing and retraining to fill now vacant positions, and lower than average productivity from disengaged, unmotivated, and frequently absent workers.

The key is to learn how to recognize what employee disengagement looks like while your company's hypothetical "canaries" are still standing upright. Once they start keeling over, so to speak, it's too late to turn to an employee survey or other assessment method to attempt to gauge their level of engagement. Looking and listening for clues is your best preemptive, and most cost-effective, measurement tool—and the first prong of your Action Plan.

Here are 12 signs that all is not well in paradise:

1. **Negativity.** Your organization is rife with complaints and whining. During a walk-through, you see and hear signs of negativity that create a toxic work environment, including disgruntled comments about the workplace and coworkers. You notice obvious or more subtle displays of emotions such as stress, apathy, anger, fear, depression, fatigue, or complacency, creating a low morale environment. Employees and managers alike blame others, bringing grievances to you without accepting any responsibility for the problem themselves, and without offering solutions.

2. **Lack of teamwork.** Rather than working collegially and cohesively in teams as is vital, employees resist collaboration, refusing to cooperate even on tasks that require group effort to succeed.

3. **Employee conflicts.** Too much time is spent "off-task" resolving employee conflicts and other individual and team problems, wasting the time of managers, HR, and fellow employees alike.

4. **Lack of interest in learning.** Employees don't show interest in, or ask for, growth opportunities or development experiences that could improve their skills in their current position and/or prepare them for promotion.

5. **Lack of initiative.** Employees avoid suggesting or initiating new projects that could contribute to the long-term success of the company. Teams don't generate ideas for new products and services, indicating that there's real disinterest in creativity and innovation.

6. **Lack of trust.** People don't come to you to share concerns or suggestions. No one asks for help or promotes ideas about how to work smarter and more efficiently because they simply feel they won't be listened to.

7. **Lack of recognition.** Both teams and individuals avoid company-related celebrations to acknowledge success of individuals, teams, or projects.

8. **Low compliance.** Rules and processes are disregarded, putting the organization at risk for legal action. Safety standards may also be ignored, leading to an increased risk for injury and lawsuits. You may see signs of theft, waste, and inventory shrinkage, suggesting operational losses are higher than what should be tolerated.

9. **Absenteeism.** Workers call in sick more often than the norm. The amount of time that people are out of the office

begins to affect their own performance, and hurt team and company productivity.

10. **Customer dissatisfaction.** In addition to hearing rumbles of customer complaints, you additionally discover that vendors are dissatisfied with their interactions with your employees. This leads to loss of customer confidence and poor relationships with vendors that could have been avoided if your employees were more engaged in nurturing these important relationships. What's more, this lack of attention to customer and vendor needs leads to poor product and service quality.

11. **High turnover.** The classic ultimate outcome of employee disengagement is that your company sheds employees faster than it should. Your organization suffers from difficulty retaining talent and even when you have the right people in place, you find that they are too easily lured to other opportunities.

12. **Difficulty attracting and developing talent.** At the end of this vicious cycle, your company not only experiences high turnover, but also has difficulty finding the right people to replace them. Once new people are in place, few aspire to take on management roles, making it difficult to develop leadership talent.

At this point we've looped back to where we started, raising a question about the best way to approach leadership development—if your business is facing any of those symptoms above, then whatever approaches you've been taking are not working. This leads us right to the next step of your action planning: If what you see around you isn't working, it's time to circle the management wagons and look within.

Tuning In to You

Why do employees become disengaged in the first place? Is it the fault of the chicken (in this case, the company) or the egg (the employee)? While you may hope that the answer to this is based on an individual's inner ennui, there's ample evidence to indicate that both engagement and disengagement start at the top - with you as the company owner or organizational executive.

Keith Ayers, CEO of Integro Leadership Institute, makes the point that most employees join a new company in an excited and engaged state. They fought for their job, won it, and are ready to get to work and make an impact. What happens next in their relationship with their managers and senior managers, or in their experiences with other company leaders, determines whether that entry level of engagement continues to flourish and grow, or whether it withers and dies like an unfed canary. Says Ayers:

> *"...since it is primarily the manager's behavior that creates the culture that employees work in, the goal of leadership development should be a measurable change in culture and employee engagement."*

That's a lot of pressure for leaders to become more emotionally aware, but those who opt out of this crucial step may find themselves dealing sooner rather than later with the 12 problems from the first prong of the action plan.

So how can you as a leader develop your emotional intelligence to the degree that it's required for understanding your own impact on employee engagement?

Here's a hint: don't hire a trainer. Internationally known psychologist Daniel Goleman, author of *Leadership: The Power of Emotional Intelligence*, has this to say about it in his book *Primal Leadership*, co-authored with Richard Boyatzis and Annie McKee:

> *"...what many organizations need aren't just one-time programs but a process built as a holistic system that permeates every layer of the organization. The best of these leadership development initiatives are based on an understanding that true change occurs through a multifaceted process that penetrates the three pivotal levels of the organization: the individuals in the organization, the teams in which they work, and the organization's culture."*

Ayers echoes this idea, noting:

> *"Many organizations make the mistake of attempting to increase emotional intelligence and leadership skills with some form of event training. A two, three or even five day training program on its own will not produce behavior change, except in the case of those rare individuals who have the self-discipline to work on what they have learned until it becomes a habit."*

So what can you do instead of falling into the same old training traps? Below are some ideas on how to avoid the wrong approaches and boost your own emotional awareness, as well as the awareness of your management team. Use these ideas strategically as the second prong of your action plan:

Don't be a robot: I know that's something I don't really have to tell you, but it is something off-the-shelf programs typically fail to address: managers and leaders have emotions, too.

If you think back to the leadership training that you participated in, most programs don't focus on that fact. On the contrary, standard approaches may advise managers to be overly cautious about their demeanor and how they express themselves, discouraging any type of emotion, with warnings such as: "Don't get upset and boil over." "Don't show your true emotions." "Be cool and stay calm."

As a result, some leaders have a tendency to avoid tough situations, simply shoving what's really going on under the table. This can be a recipe for disaster and, sooner or later, the emotions that were shunted aside will resurface even more forcefully, often when they're least wanted. When that does happen your frustrations can be directed toward someone you didn't intend to receive them, like your boss or family.

Most training programs also disregard the variety of work styles and communication styles that different leaders possess. Teams generally leave such training programs armed with guidelines and processes that fail to take into account the range of emotions and individual distinctions that make up each person more holistically as a leader.

When leaders avoid bringing emotion to the table, or when they feel disempowered to appropriately express their emotions, they risk demotivating their people, and this can, of course, negatively impact workplace culture, employee engagement, and retention. In order for employees to be fully engaged, they need to feel that they are following leaders who inspire them emotionally. You don't get inspiration in a box—it only comes by practicing authentic leadership.

Don't shun conflict: Being an effective leader means knowing how to deal with conflict on a variety of levels.

When leadership development is done incorrectly, unsuspecting managers and leaders may find themselves walking into conflicts unequipped to handle them effectively. They may push too hard in trying to mediate, instead creating the possibility of retaliation from their employees. They may try the "buddy" approach to their direct reports rather than serving in a leadership role, and get walked on by their staff.

The emotionally unaware leader may prefer to avoid conflict and ignore signs of "sick canaries" in the office. That's because, in the short term, conflict can be emotionally draining, and all the more so if leaders internalize their feelings rather than taking the initiative to approach situations head-on. Remember that not all conflict is bad and, in fact, it can force leaders to face colleagues and employees more honestly.

Development programs that don't reflect this can leave leaders high and dry by failing to provide customized skills in negotiating conflict situations. Leadership development that takes the whole person—and specific whole situations—into account can produce better emotional outcomes for all involved. In the long run, this isn't just about feeling good, it's about saving business relationships and jobs. So take a customized approach to learning how to handle the unique conflicts that you face, and then handle them.

Acknowledge the pressure: Traditional development methods often are structured with the expectation that managers will quickly and easily find a way to markedly apply what they learned.

What that completely ignores is the apprehension and anxiety that many managers feel if they believe they're not applying what they're supposed to have learned. The obvious consequences are that this places a large amount of pressure on managers and leaders to perform, which can often backfire.

Typically in such programs, leaders are given some simplistic yet so-called utopian a clever acronym or five-step framework to follow, and leave these canned sessions with a false sense that all they must do to build stronger teams is put this simplified framework into place and their employees will naturally follow suit. Wrong!

The reality is that your employees won't know they are supposed to follow some three or five or seven-step process unless you take the time to show them how to do so in a way that's truly meaningful.

More likely, the framework will die in its training binder, dusty on a shelf and lost in the shuffle of what needs to be done today (or yesterday).

When what you've learned in training fails to deliver results, as a leader, you can feel even more alone. You might even start to self-doubt your abilities, fueling conflicts and fear of failure—especially if the training design makes participants feel like their shortcomings are being singled out for "fixing."

None of these things will lead to better employee engagement or team building, which were among the goals of the training. In fact, it's clear to see that training methods like these can cause the opposite results from those desired.

Seek the truth: Though the conventional image of a business leader suggests someone strong and self-contained at the head of the pack, leading can also mean experiencing loneliness.

In small to mid-size businesses, or departments in a corporatation, leadership teams may consist of a handful of people and supportive peers may be numbered, and here leaders may be more likely to feel isolated than invincible.

Leadership also lends itself to this emotional truth: you are treated differently as a manager, separated from the pack and stuck in the middle or at the top. When the teams supporting you—whether from above or below—don't mirror your urgency or give the same amount of effort that you do, it's easy to feel like no one quite understands you.

Effective leadership development needs to take these emotional realities into account and not offer up stock answers. As a leader, if you receive generalized advice in a program that doesn't fit your situation or your needs, push back and demand better. And fully expect your employees to do the same.

Here's the take-home:

> *You can take steps to boost your emotional intelligence and ward off employee disengagement by the simple act of switching out of traditional training programs, instead implementing true development initiatives.*

The next two chapters will add fuel to the fire about why it's so important to link development to strategy as a precursor to creating any developmental plan, designing program content based on your organization's current challenges—and Part III of the book will show you how to do it.

CHAPTER 8

PRODUCTIVITY COSTS

THE TRICKLE-DOWN EFFECT OF POOR LEADERSHIP DEVELOPMENT

"It is important to remember that leadership development is not just about developing leaders—it is about creating a culture of performance… Leadership development creates a magnet for high-performers and fosters a high-performance organization."

–Bersin & Associates

Perfect may be the enemy of the good. But believing things are good enough when they aren't can be just as problematic. Do you feel satisfied with the status quo of your company's level of leadership skills and performance, even if signals are telling you otherwise? If so, it's time to wake up and smell the profit loss.

When you do things wrong with your company's leadership development, it sets a vicious cycle in motion, and it all starts with the canary—emotional costs clue you into the fact that something's not working. But it doesn't end there and far from it.

The emotional costs of employee disengagement lead to something much worse from the perspective of the business owner: a kick in your company's collective productivity. And it doesn't end there, either. As you'll see in Chapter 9, ultimately, your company's finances will take the biggest hit at the end of this dysfunctional process loop.

To provide context for understanding the full impact to your bottom line when leadership development goes wrong, let's first examine the intermediate step in this sad scenario: productivity costs.

THE SLIPPERY SLOPE

Are you ready to apply what you learned in the last chapter? As the person who cares the most about your business, I'm sure you're now ready to take heed of the canary's warning warbles, which would register the initial signs of your employees' distress. At least I hope you are and if not you now know where you're going to end up.

Whether it's shoddy teamwork, visibly low morale, or absenteeism that tips you off, there could well be plenty of indications early on that your leadership development was not up to snuff, and your most valuable assets were suffering the consequences.

If you ignore these red flags, you unfortunately move your entire company toward stage two of this workplace disease, propelling into motion significant hits to the productivity level of your teams. When people lag that means companies lag, so if your people aren't producing to the best of their ability, then neither is your company. This is why the emotional signs that something's gone wrong in your workplace are so critical—if you can catch problems at the early stage, you can avoid much worse damage down the road.

For argument's sake, let's assume you *didn't* listen to your chirping friend and now find yourself noticing more than just grumpy employees. As a reminder, it's going to be things like:

- Lower growth rates
- Higher turnover
- Decreased customer satisfaction
- Lower productivity

Let's look at each of these elements in turn and find out why this happens before we explore how to fix it.

GROWING NOWHERE

It can be hard to invest resources in developing employees and leaders without truly grasping the impact of such actions to your bottom line. Therefore, the first thing to understand is that since employees are generally the largest chunk of any company's financials, a lazy approach to leadership development will soon begin to reveal quantifiable problems.

Research in *Harvard Business Review* by Laurie Bassi, a former economics professor at Georgetown University, reveals the degree to which proper leadership development affects company growth and productivity. Bassi found that when leaders don't provide feedback, fail to eliminate barriers, aren't open to new ideas, fail to inspire confidence, and withhold information from their employees, their organizations experience lower overall performance and growth than those that do.

The study compared the average compound annual income growth rate over three years for a number of sales offices. It found that the growth rate scores for offices that ranked high in leadership development (or human capital management) ranged up to 130 percent higher than the growth rate for offices with lower scores. In a separate study of 750 large public firms, Bassi found that companies with high investment in leadership development provided shareholder returns that were three times better than companies with weaker investments in human capital.

BEATING A PATH TO THE WRONG DOOR

You saw a preview of this one in Chapter 7. When employees truly disengage from your workplace, you'll hear the sound of feet stampeding to your door—the exit. People will always come and go, but if your company is experiencing serious trouble retaining your top talent, it's going to hurt your company's productivity and eventually impact corporate financial performance.

We explored how expensive it is to replace different levels of employees throughout the recruiting cycle—30 to 50 percent of annual salary is a conservative estimate for more junior employees, and the percentage skyrockets when replacing more specialized positions.

If you're dealing with these costs, then look within. Poor leadership development is the elephant in the room behind an exodus of talent from any organization. A leader's ability to provide direction, feedback, and support is key to their groups' job satisfaction and productivity.

The Saratoga Institute found that over 30 percent of turnover costs tie directly to poor leadership and management practices. Anonymous exit interview research revealed that, in many cases, employees leave bad managers, not bad companies. Employees in the study identified the following reasons—all related to leadership competencies—that lurk behind their decision to leave an organization:

- Lack of support/respect from the supervisor
- Supervisor's poor leadership skills
- Supervisor's poor employee relations
- Failure of the supervisor to recognize employee's work
- Incompetence of the supervisor

It can't be underestimated how much productivity gets impacted by this reverse stampede, and the top-line impact is that companies with high employee turnover have a harder time finding and keeping customers, increasing quality, and pursuing growth ventures. Nextera research has suggested this can add up to a 50 percent cost as a percentage of industry earnings—that's a lot of lost opportunity.

On the flip side, Bersin & Associates found that companies that take a strategic approach to leadership development are nearly 75 percent more effective at improving overall employee retention.

SERVICE SLUMP

I'm sure you can see where this is going now. Poor leadership development affects your employees' performance while they're working for you, or leads them to seek greener pastures working for others. If your employees aren't providing top service to your customers—or because of high turnover are not consistently available to them, presenting a constant rotation of new faces as your company's front—it's your customers who are next down the chain to suffer.

Research in *The Harvard Business Review* by Rucci et al revealed that the difference between "average" and "exceptional" customer satisfaction levels translates to an almost 4 percent reduction in annual revenue growth for the typical organization. And if you're thinking that a less than 5 percent loss isn't that much, recognize that even a low percentage reduction can result in a potential revenue loss of hundreds of thousands of dollars for organizations that generate $10 million or more a year. Studies by *The Ken Blanchard Companies* suggest that less-than-optimal leadership practices can cost companies up to 7 percent of total annual sales.

How can you prevent bleeding this cash? Leadership effectiveness is the start of the chain. Rucci's research concluded that leadership practices leading to better employee satisfaction scores result in better customer satisfaction scores as well, translating directly into bottom-line impact. Blanchard's studies have shown that improving leadership skills such as delegation, directive behavior, and feedback and support add up to a 3.8 percent improvement in levels of customer satisfaction. What's more, this same research suggests that better leadership development can boost corporate revenue growth by close to 2 percent.

Some years ago, Virgin founder Richard Branson spoke to the UK's Institute of Directors and he talked about the leadership he instills, from the very top, in his management teams. Quite simply, it's another equation that reads: happy people = happy customers = happy shareholders.

The right leadership development is the shining star behind the coveted trio of employee engagement, customer satisfaction, and organizational success. And Blanchard's research has confirmed that they're all connected:

- Effective leadership development can predict employee engagement
- Employee engagement can predict customer satisfaction
- Customer satisfaction can predict organizational vitality

Because of this trickle-down effect, the key for business leaders is to ensure that the right thing is trickling down. You want to avoid putting the opposite wheels in motion: ineffective leadership predicting employee disengagement predicting customer dissatisfaction predicting...

THE ULTIMATE RESULT

...lower productivity.

The now obvious outcome of this negative series of events can only be a downward spiral and dispiriting drag in employee productivity, which ultimately affects overall company performance. Leaders drive performance—or inhibit it—by how they communicate goals and objectives, demonstrate values, and influence behavior. Leveraging your leadership team's influence by investing in their development can substantially impact your company's bottom line.

Countless studies over the past two decades have proven the connection between the quality of leadership and employee productivity. Research published in 2011 by Blanchard suggests that direct-report productivity might be improved up to 12 percent simply by improving leadership and management practices. Blanchard has estimated that the majority of companies operate somewhere between a 5 and 10 percent productivity deficit that could be corrected simply by implementing the right kind of leadership development.

A survey of 1,300 private-sector companies conducted by *Proudfoot Consulting* identified three major culprits behind employees not working at their full potential, and surprise! Inadequate management was one of them. The other drag factors pinpointed were also related to dysfunctional leadership: insufficient planning and control, and poor working morale. On average, the study found that because of leadership gone wrong, over 40 percent of work time on average is unproductive.

LEADERSHIP "GONE RIGHT" HOLDS THE KEY

Everything hinges on leadership. As a company leader or CEO you're at the start of a chain reaction that ultimately leads to your company's success or failure. So what can you do? The answer is to go back to the basics of what it takes to run a successful business, and remember the importance of taking care of your employees.

Leadership development "done right" equals smart business. It leads to employees who are genuinely committed to their employers and jobs, and thus are more productive. This spins the merry-go-round in the right direction toward better customer support and company profitability.

Investing in your people is what builds cooperation, trust, talent, engagement, innovation, organizational learning, and yes: productivity. According to Gallup, engaged or committed employees usually take fewer sick days and generate an average of 43 percent more revenue. Employee engagement matters to business owners because more productive employees lead to enhanced customer service that drives customer satisfaction—and company performance.

Some strategies that can help leaders create a high-performing work environment include:

Ask the right questions: First and foremost, leaders must determine whether their employees understand the goals of the company and their specific role in achieving those goals.

You can learn to ask the right questions of your employees from the outset of projects to assess whether your people are there with you or not. By doing so, you can find out quickly what each employee needs to be most productive.

Set clear expectations: Once employees understand what they need to do, they still can benefit from leadership direction on how to do it.

When people don't receive the support required to complete their job successfully, the result is wasted time, poor quality, and expensive rework. Your employees need a clear plan for accomplishing the company's goals. Leaders must ensure that their employees have everything they need—from tools and direction to resources and support—to perform at their best.

Provide motivation: Leaders can, and should, make a big difference in your company's engagement by ensuring that employees stay motivated and inspired.

This often comes down to taking the time to understand each team and employee, and assessing their motivation to work on a particular project. Like all the topics we've covered, motivation can't be solved with a quick-fix training solution, but instead it requires a customized approach based on your company's specific culture and the personalities of the individuals on your teams.

Look for the blocks: You may have provided your engaged employees with goals, tools, and motivation, but if there are systemic obstacles or organizational bottlenecks hampering workflow, employees may soon grow discouraged.

You need to work hard to eliminate unnecessary paperwork, unproductive meetings, administrative burdens, insufficient resources, and tools or systems that create more problems than they solve. Some off-the-shelf training programs may, of course, fall into this category!

Your leaders should recognize and address these barriers to optimum productivity. Take it upon yourself as the one in charge to ensure that your employees experience a work environment free from suboptimal processes and other organizational ills.

GO HARD OR GO HOME

There's no need to beat this to death, but once you accept the fact that you'll end up with decreased productivity when you fail to take a smart approach to leadership development, you'll see that the only way to run your company is to ensure that you engage in the types of development opportunities discussed in earlier chapters. Hint: if it comes packaged as a premade training binder, that's not the right kind!

You need to remember that the solution that looks the easiest is not always the best. The temptation for business owners is always to grab at the shiny box packaged up with a neat bow that promises to solve any and all corporate problems—no matter how big or small your company is, and regardless of your organization's individual factors. Don't pick up that box. But don't do "nothing", either.

Since the research described above shows that many organizations are forfeiting dollars that amount to 7 percent of their total annual sales due to the choices that they're making around leadership development, clearly something must be done. But when leadership development goes right, then that "something" will necessarily vary depending on the particular challenges that your company faces.

A custom-designed leadership development initiative may temporarily be more difficult and disruptive than what's in the box—but it offers you much better odds for a lasting solution. As Blanchard points out, failing to implement an optimum leadership development strategy can cost far more in time, resources, dollars, and training than taking care of what really needs to be done.

Smart leaders will always try to avoid excessive costs in tough times, but investing in your company's ability to increase its performance capacity isn't an excessive cost—it's more like a survival strategy. Research shows that leadership development pays off by driving a culture of performance: both employee performance and bottom-line financial performance.

According to the Center for Creative Leadership (CCL), a wide range of studies have proven: "Organizations that invest in leadership development perform better than those that don't." If this doesn't sound like you, but you're ambivalent about investing in leadership development, then maybe your company's issue isn't cost avoidance, but that:

- You haven't taken the time to do a true needs assessment;
- You've failed to align corporate goals and objectives with business outcomes;

- You haven't measured and evaluated the performance and results of the shiny-box programs versus custom leadership development.

If so, that's a mistake, as research firm Bersin & Associates states:

> *"The message is clear—leadership development matters. It is hard to find a company which has survived many economic cycles that does not have a [sophisticated] leadership development strategy in place. While it may take many years to develop and refine, the results clearly pay off."*

What's more, CCL's report emphasizes that the importance increases for companies to invest in leadership development during economic downturns so that businesses don't just survive, but become stronger than their competition. Your productivity goals must go beyond merely wanting to stay afloat; they should be about thriving.

Regardless of the cause of your current predicament, if you're still not sure what your own company's approach to leadership development might look like, never fear. In Part III, I've outlined a four-step process that you can use as a starting point to tailor-make your own development plan.

Here's the take-home:

> *You're the leader; you set the tone for your organization's productivity, for better or for worse. Maximum benefit occurs only when your company's leadership development inspires employee engagement that leads to better customer support, and ultimately increased productivity. Suboptimal leadership practices can leave substantial sums on the table each year, leading to a drain in your company's financial performance.*

CHAPTER 9

FINANCIAL COSTS

PAYING THROUGH THE NOSE FOR BAD LEADERSHIP DEVELOPMENT

It always all boils down to money, doesn't it? Every consequence mentioned so far—from the emotional costs of disengaged employees who don't perform at their best, to the resulting productivity costs of this lack of commitment in your teams, which ultimately affects your customers (or potential customers who you lose through this process)—matters in large part to you as a business owner or executive responsible for the bottom line. Whatever your situation, it simply means less money in your pocket.

Yes, we care about our people and want them to feel excited and engaged to work for us. But is wanting our employees' happiness enough to jump through all of the hoops necessary to get it? Probably not, if at the end of the day, your business doesn't make enough money.

WHY MONEY MATTERS

Let's get real about this: you're in business to make money. So why not do what it takes to ensure that your business will do as well, as possible financially? If you discovered that doing a tap dance while chanting in Cantonese would ensure that your business would be 5-10 percent more financially successful, you'd do it, right? Well you'd give it a go!

The reality, of course, is that you don't have to do a tap dance or learn a foreign language. What helps companies become more profitable is simply having the right leadership development in place so that employees naturally become more engaged. Something being "right" means it's measurable and leadership development being quantified is not just about HR checking "provide continuing professional education" off a list.

Countless studies over the past two decades have pointed to connections between effective leadership practices and improved corporate financial performance. Way back in 1995, a Rutgers University large-scale study of nearly a thousand companies noted a correlation that was statistically significant between development strategies and the firms' bottom lines.

More recently, along with Bassi's research mentioned earlier that showed average annual growth rates climbed up to 130 percent higher in companies that prioritized leadership development, a study in *Chief Learning Officer* suggests bottom lines can be substantially raised—and profits perhaps doubled—by grooming leaders who remove employees' obstacles to productivity and inspire better performance.

As we discussed in the last chapter, some studies have shown companies that have only average customer satisfaction ratings—the result of employees who aren't fully engaged—will experience nearly 4 percent less annual revenue growth than companies with exceptional customer satisfaction. When Gallup reviewed an analysis of data from more than 150 organizations, it found that companies with engaged employees have 3.9 percent higher earnings per share growth rate compared with less engaged companies. Other studies have set this number higher, citing a loss of up to 7 percent of total yearly sales that can be traced back to poor leadership practices.

Consider again the $300 billion that Gallup estimates as the level of lost productivity from employee disengagement in the U.S. alone—that's a very high price to pay for something that can be fixed by changing your approach to leadership development.

GRANDMA KNOWS BEST

Perhaps not surprisingly, I'm a fan of Ken Blanchard who has developed an entire business case for leadership development. Like me, he has had the experience of trying to convince CEOs and business owners that investing in proper leadership development will help save them money—or make them more money—in the long run.

Often, top execs and business owners alike are inclined to focus only on what's right in front of them—the initial cost of a new initiative—without researching to see whether and how soon their investment will pay off. My grandma would call this approach "pennywise and pound foolish." Will integrating leadership development that really works cost something on the front end? Absolutely—what effective strategy is free? But will doing so result in better financial results for your company in the long run, maybe even sooner than you think? Most definitely. It's not an expense with no return, it's highly measurable investment.

You don't have to take my word for it, either—Blanchard's research has already proven it. He conducted an analysis of over 200 companies with the use of a tool that he calls the "Cost of Doing Nothing Calculator." He discovered, not surprisingly, that each year companies fail to incorporate true leadership development practices, the more it ends up hurting them financially.

Blanchard's the one who discovered that lack of leadership development leads to a loss of around 7 percent of total sales for a typical organization, and that *the average company is saying goodbye to over a million a year that can be traced right back to their leadership practices.* Just read those italicized words again. That yearly income drain hurts a lot more than typical start-up costs, yet business owners often worry more that setting up proper leadership development will be too expensive and time consuming. So do your homework, take a tip from grandma, and prioritize pounds over pennies.

WHAT'S YOUR NUMBER?

It's all well and good to point to general percentages for typical companies, but I don't want to simply suggest that you settle for "everyman's" numbers when a custom-tailored formula for *your* particular company is what you really need.

Fortunately, there's a way to determine exactly how much cash you're bleeding by failing to adequately address leadership development in your business, and that's by using Blanchard's aforementioned "Cost of Doing Nothing Calculator" which is available free from his website: **www.kenblanchard.com** and you can find this ROI calculator on the "Leading Research" page.

The simple tool allows you to plug in some numbers related to your company's specific employee turnover, customer satisfaction, and employee productivity, and you'll be presented on the spot with your company's very own "Total Cost of Doing Nothing" number.

Here's how it works:

Step 1: Employee Turnover

Let's say you have 20 employees with an average salary of $50,000, and your current turnover rate is 20 percent. When you enter these figures into the Cost of Doing Nothing Calculator, you'll discover—no doubt to your horror—that your company's annual cost of employee turnover is $100,000.

But the financial pain doesn't end there.

Step 2: Customer Satisfaction

As we discussed earlier, high customer satisfaction springs from your investment in leadership development in a chain reaction, but let's image you've not started yet. If we tell the calculator that your company's annual sales are $500,000, your current customer satisfaction rate is 75 percent, but your desired customer satisfaction rate is 100 percent, then it reveals that your yearly cost of underdeveloped customer satisfaction is $48,076. These costs are really adding up, and we haven't finished the exercise yet.

Step 3: Employee Productivity

Blanchard finds that most organizations he works with estimate that their employees are only about 70 percent as productive as they could be. So let's take your specific numbers: if your approximate annual sales are $500,000 and you estimate that your current productivity rate is a little bit higher than the average—say 80 percent—but you would like to reach 100 percent productivity, then you can add another $100,000 to your total number for annual cost of underdeveloped productivity.

So if these were your company's numbers, then your "Total Cost of Doing Nothing" would be a whopping $248,076—almost half of your annual sales!

WHY YOU SHOULD CARE

Again, it all comes down to money. If there's something you can do for your business to save substantial sums rather than losing them as in the examples above, you'll do it, if you care about the long-term success of your business.

So how much could strong leadership development help you turn your numbers around? The calculator also automatically computes what you could save with improved leadership practices and, in the example above, this comes out as a saving of $9,000 in employee turnover.

This sum is based on research by The Saratoga Institute, which suggests that poor leadership practices are behind a minimum of 9 percent of an organization's turnover, and possibly as much as 33 percent. Erring on the low side, by multiplying the estimated turnover costs ($100,000 in our example) by 9 percent, the calculator arrives at your projected savings in this area.

Now let's look at how you can save money by making your customers feel better. Research published in the *Harvard Business Review* highlights that when customers aren't satisfied with what your employees are doing for them, your bottom line suffers. Yet for every 1.3 percent increase your company sees in its customer satisfaction scores, you'll net a .5 percent increase in sales.

So in our current example, by multiplying annual sales ($500,000) by the 1.46 percent increase that Blanchard estimates you could achieve with better leadership development, you end up with another $7,300 in savings.

Last but far from least, let's look at how tuning up your leadership development can save you in the area of productivity. Blanchard cites a study of 1,500 people (300 managers and 1,200 employees) that revealed at least a 5 percent increase (and in some cases as high as 12 percent) in employee productivity on the heels of putting leadership development initiatives in place.

Even if we take the lower number, when we multiply 5 percent by current annual sales of $500,000, the Calculator reveals very significant savings of $25,000 in productivity. Put all that together for our hypothetical company and there are substantial savings of $41,300. Use the calculator to crunch your own numbers, and try not to cry when you see how much money you're losing by failing to address deficiencies in your approach to leadership development.

WHEN TO GET GOING

I've heard the excuses before:

> *"I can't invest in leadership development in this economy."*
>
> *"It's not the right time—I'll wait until my business is doing better."*
>
> *"Why not just skip leadership development and try this quick lunch and learn instead?"*

But guess what? The Center for Creative Leadership (CCL) reports that investments in leadership development made during challenging economic times yield the best ROI. According to CCL, research on Fortune 500 companies has found that it's even more important for companies to support their leadership during a recession than during smoother economic conditions.

And if you can give this vote of confidence in your leadership by providing them with the development opportunities that they need, the payoff will be that your business will emerge from the tough times stronger than your competition.

BITING THE BULLET FOR YOUR BUSINESS

I hope I've made the point loud and clear that there is a significant business case for prioritizing leadership development in your company. This isn't just about wanting to provide people with learning opportunities or have happier employees, though these things will likely turn out to be positive side effects of doing development right.

As *Harvard Business Review* has reported, as Gallup has proven, as Blanchard has studied: your approach to leadership development really does make a difference to the corporate coin count. Sub-optimal leadership training isn't just a waste of time—it costs companies like yours millions a year by ruining retention, productivity, and customer satisfaction.

A study of a large financial services firm published in *Training Industry Quarterly* found that direct reports raised the bar on their productivity up to 12 percent when their managers received properly structured leadership development support—and put their new skills into practice.

Corporate change is never easy, as we discussed back in Chapter 3. It may seem like making the modifications necessary to get your leadership team up to speed will be too disruptive and expensive to be worth it. But what the research has revealed is that you are taking a much bigger financial risk *not* investing in your company's leaders.

Are you willing to let an average of 7 percent of your total annual sales slip away because you didn't take the initiative when you needed to? Using the same current and target performance levels as the example above, I reworked the numbers for a company with 1,000 employees and sales of $5,000,000—sounds impressive doesn't it—and the "doing nothing" cost came out at a staggering $6,384,615!

Here's the take-home:

> *Failing to invest in leadership development doesn't just hurt your leaders—it hurts your company's bottom line. As a business owner or senior executive, you can't afford the financial costs of leadership training gone wrong.*

You don't have to rely on case studies or other entrepreneurs' failures—you can crunch your own numbers to see just how much money you're losing each year by taking a complacent approach to developing your top people.

PART III

Learn to FUEL Your Organization to the Next Level

CHAPTER 10
HOW TO RUN ON FUEL, NOT FUMES

It's all led up to this: what to do about leadership development gone wrong. You now understand clearly how you may have led your company astray by taking an ineffective approach to solving organizational performance issues.

You've seen how some things that many companies try to manage—such as change, time, and stress—just can't be managed. You've also learned about exactly what's at stake for leaders who insist on trying to manage the unmanageable through "out of the box" solutions that claim to help any company, but in fact help no company because they aren't targeted at anyone's specific problems.

What's at stake is the success or failure of your entire organization. Backed up by significant research, I've shown you that ineffective development leads to disengaged employees and a cascade of consequences that follow, ending in the lowered productivity of your workforce and decreased corporate financial performance.

This is indeed a depressing thought for any business owner or corporate leader. But I haven't written this book to simply show you the problems with your current approach and leave you holding the bag, wondering what to do about it. I wrote this book to provide you with workable solutions, and I had to paint such a black picture first to help you accept that my ideas are the ones worth listening to.

DEVELOPMENT BLUEPRINT

The rest of this book will provide you with a blueprint for how to link your company's development objectives to your corporate strategy as a precursor to creating any leadership developmental plan. The key is to ensure that *your* program content is designed based on *your* organization's current challenges. Sorry, but I really can't say that enough.

So the good news is that you don't need to figure out how to do this alone; I'm here to guide you through the process. In my work over the years with business owners, I've developed a system to help leaders break out of their training ruts and improve their leadership competencies, solving the problem of disengaged employees and protecting their bottom lines.

As you no doubt expected, that way is through leaving classic "training" behind, focusing instead on real development of competencies, skills, and behaviors needed for effective, authentic leadership. The strategy and culture of a company should influence the nature of any leadership development program in order for it to be effective, not some totally untailored "package" in fancy binders.

To accomplish this, companies must learn to lead change, not manage change. This can be done through a four-stage process called **FUEL**, which stands for: **F**ind, **U**tilize, **E**ngage, **L**ead. Okay, so it's got an acronym and sounds structured, but it needs to be. It's what goes on "inside" each stage that's important, so let me explain—in some ways the next heading says it all.

A TAILORED APPROACH

Unlike step-based trainings that are artificially imposed with no true substance behind them, these four stages—a much broader concept—provide a comprehensive program for all of your organizational performance needs. The stages can be adapted to address many key areas of challenge—including change, time, and stress—to produce solutions that are truly right for your business.

As I hope you have determined from my emphasis in earlier chapters, **FUEL** is based on the underlying principle of determining the particular competencies that *your* employees need assistance with, rather than slapping on a "one size fits all" approach—I think I've mentioned enough that a generic "best practices" approach won't work.

To properly influence company culture in a way that results in stronger leadership and better engagement, you must first understand exactly what's going on in *your* organization. That's where the **FUEL** process comes in.

PIECING IT ALL TOGETHER

FUEL is all about how you as a business leader can help catapult your organization from merely functional to truly viable, ensuring that tasks and responsibilities are completed with efficiency, on target and on budget. For your organization to go from good to great, those same tasks and responsibilities need to be completed as part of an overall plan, focused on long-term success and growth.

Approaching training challenges piecemeal, outside of the larger context of corporate strategy, will not bring your organization the success that you seek. Neither will relying on inconsistent employee surveys, which often end up filed away, never to be seen again. **FUEL** is the opposite of these methods. It's a comprehensive program to address all of your organizational performance needs in conjunction with one another.

No matter where you are with your leadership development program—whether you've been able to identify some specific challenges that you are certain need fixing, or know that you need help to get to the next level, but aren't sure what areas to focus on—**FUEL** offers the chance for a customized solution.

Here's an overview of how it works:

Find

If there's one point that I've tried to make in this book, it's that all training attempts are useless when they aren't based on the specific needs of your company. The Find stage is what allows you to gather the right information to make informed development decisions.

During the Find stage, the **FUEL** process helps guide your company's leadership to:

- Pinpoint critical success factors based on your organization's unique needs;
- Develop a competency library;
- Identify behavioral indicators;
- Define performance measures to plan next steps related to learning outcomes.

"Find" is really all about becoming a scientist of your own business. When you take a look around your business and your industry, can you identify what will it take to get to the next level? Do you need innovative products or solutions? How about the ability to react to changes in the market? Maybe you need to take a risk and instead of being a "me-too company", you do what it takes to become the leader of the pack. The Find stage is also about discovering what's missing in your industry, and seeing if you can re-tool your organization to take advantage of a gap.

The Find stage is not just about unearthing problems, however. It's also about defining the skills and competencies you need to meet the needs of what you uncover. This process needs to be very specific to be effective.

For example, you can't just say "We need be more effective at communication" because *everyone* has a perception that they are communicating well to a certain degree. You need to define exactly what effective communication looks like in your company—what are the behavioral indicators? Does it mean working collaboratively—internally across departments and externally to customers, suppliers, and vendors? And how would you rate that skill or competency in your company today?

The answers to questions like these are what you use to define performance measures to plan your next steps related to learning outcomes. No one can ignore the old adage of "needing measures to manage", so Find is the first crucial stage in your company's unique path to leadership development approaches that are really going to work.

Utilize

Stopping after the Find stage would be like running a quarter of a marathon and dropping out. The point of identifying unique success factors for your company is to use that information to design customized strategies that address specific organizational initiatives—from hiring plans to succession planning—which you identified in the Find stage. That's what the Utilize stage is all about.

Even customized strategies won't work, though, if you don't have the right people in place to accomplish your goals, or if there is there a gap in either your employees' skills or their behavior. So Utilize refers to figuring out the best ways to use your existing resources to tackle the problems you've identified—or, if you discover in the Find stage that you are lacking resources in certain areas, strategizing other ways to fill those needs.

For example, you may have great people but not enough capacity to get the job done. In that case, you'd need to figure out what is mission-critical and what can be outsourced or pushed down to other areas such as shipping, maintenance, human resources, or accounting. If the activity in question is not a core part of your business, then you won't want to place your best people on these tasks. The task may be essential, but if it's not critical to how you bring in revenue, then it needs to be considered for other resources.

Another way to utilize existing resources might be to tap into the knowledge based within your company. Maybe you have someone who is the "guru" regarding a piece of software. Maybe one of your managers knows a process from soup to nuts. These are the individuals who should partner with whoever—internal staff or learning consultants—who are working on the creation of job aids or other training materials. In other words, instead of having someone come in and roll out pre-prepared training for your people, let your people be the engine that helps create and generate truly tailored development resources.

As suggested with the mention of learning consultants, now that the needs have been initially determined and tailored, don't stop with your employees when considering what you can utilize, since external vendors or suppliers might have something to offer at this stage. Then there's the possibility of partnerships with other businesses. Any business that is not a competitor might prove a valuable alliance for creation of a cohort, user group, or roundtable—let the Utilize stage encourage you get creative and expansive in your thinking about how to build a better business.

Engage

We've spent a lot of time in earlier chapters discussing the critical importance of employee engagement to the overall financial success of your company. So now it is time to stop talking and rally the troops to understand where your employees are coming from. In the Engage stage, you focus on surveying the current level of engagement in your company—not just employee satisfaction, but true engagement. Where are the hearts and minds of your most important assets for propelling your company forward?

This stage involves measuring what your employees value—as well as their satisfaction and mindset—to determine the most effective channels for communicating each person's role in a more productive, sustainable organization. Again, what gets measured gets done, so these engagement-related measurements are crucial to determining the exact direction in which to tailor your development initiatives.

Gauging the current state of engagement is not enough, however. Engagement today does not imply that you'll still have the same level of engagement tomorrow. Once you're aware of the current state of engagement, you need to develop ways to keep employees engaged in the future. This involves experimenting with different methods of engaging the entire organization for the long haul.

Engagement is another area where leaders often hope for best practices, but generate your own ideas and approaches before you hare off trying to compare your organization to other companies. This can be a good thing though as you seek to fine tune what you're doing because, if your heart is in the right place, engagement is hard to screw up.

Improving engagement is about having everyone on board, and employees want to feel like they can impact the bigger picture. While there is no need for company picnics every week, a key aspect about this stage is seeking to create a culture of fun, but making it your own.

Lead

The Lead stage ties the three earlier stages together, ensuring that you have a team of leaders who continuously support the mission, vision, and goals that your organization has identified in different areas—for example, in relation to change, time, and stress. This stage helps you maintain a more rewarding, productive, and profitable business by continuing to evaluate and identify areas for growth.

Obviously, that's a short way to explain a very comprehensive concept of a leadership development methodology, but I'll expand on each stage more in the coming chapters, providing examples of how you might consider using each stage to **FUEL** your organization to greater success.

Here's the take-home:

> *FUEL is where the rubber hits the road in your company's organizational development planning. The four-stage process of Find, Utilize, Engage, and Lead provides you with a blueprint for how to link your company's development to your corporate strategy as a precursor to creating any developmental plan.*
>
> *By ensuring that your program content is designed based on your organization's current challenges, you can help catapult your organization from merely functional to truly viable, ensuring that tasks and responsibilities are completed with efficiency, on target and on budget.*

CHAPTER 11
FINDING REAL SOLUTIONS

Why is the "**F**" stage of the **FUEL** process so important? The best way to understand this is to examine the wrong way that people often approach problems. Leadership training gone wrong often begins with off-base problem-solving at the start of the process. I'll explain what I mean.

Let's say I'm at an off-site meeting with you, and I complain about my allergies. How might you respond to me? For many people, the natural response when confronted with any problem is to try to figure out how to alleviate its symptoms. So when someone complains of allergies, chances are you might suggest a symptom-based remedy.

Perhaps you'd mention that a friend had success with a certain allergy medication, or you'd speculate on whether I should avoid eating certain foods, or offer me a tissue. While these are all nice gestures, the fact is, you'd be providing me with possible solutions before finding out what's really behind my problem.

Maybe my symptoms weren't the result of allergies at all, but were because I was unknowingly coming down with a cold. Maybe I'd just come from another meeting with someone wearing heavy perfume, and I'm allergic to perfume. Maybe I already take allergy medication but had forgotten to bring it to the conference. Without finding out more about why I was experiencing my particular symptoms, any suggested solutions could be a waste of time, or worse, they could cause other side effects by failing to treat the right problem (for example by giving an allergy medication to a cold sufferer).

While this example may seem mundane, it provides an accurate analogy of how many business owners approach problem-solving in their organizations. They identify a challenge—whether it's productivity or difficulty managing change—and then look to their teams or third parties to jump to solutions before gathering any data whatsoever about what is really going on.

At this stage, many professionals will start offering ideas without asking additional questions to get at the root of the conundrum. That's how some leadership teams end up investing in another lunch and learn or time management course that absorbs company resources without providing any long-term ROI.

BEHIND THE ALLERGIES

The Find stage of **FUEL** is what allows companies to investigate what's behind their corporate allergies. Something specific is making your leadership team suffer, your employees sniffle, or your bottom line wheeze. The Find stage gives you a framework to figure out what that specific something is. It does so by opening the dialogue to additional questions that *truly* get to the bottom of what's happening in your organization.

To exemplify how this works, let's continue the analogy above. What if, instead of immediately suggesting that I might benefit from the most popular "off the shelf" medication, you decided to ask me some questions about my condition? You might have then found out that I'm a long-time allergy and asthma sufferer, and that I'd been using an inhaler for my symptoms since I was a kid. On this business trip, I'd forgotten my inhaler, so I was planning to take a trip to the pharmacy after the meeting to get what I needed. So instead of trying to be an expert pharmacist, the simple offer of a tissue might have been the right initial answer.

Likewise, when a business owner tells me about where their organization is trying to go, yet it's clear they're stuck somewhere, I don't jump to suggesting a series of classes that might help. Even if the classes are good ones, even if research has shown these are the top classes for solving certain types of problems, I don't have enough information yet to recommend them effectively. Even if these classes were the right ones for your employees, the order that they're taken might make a difference. Maybe your teams need to improve their communication skills before they address productivity issues, or vice-versa.

This is really about front-end analysis, a concept that's discussed in detail by Dana Gaines Robinson and James Robinson, authors of *Performance Consulting: A Practical Guide for HR and Learning Professionals*. Before you engage in improving performance, you need to conduct an assessment of why performance is lagging. That assessment may take the form of a needs analysis, performance analysis, or gap analysis—whatever term you use, the point is that you need to thoroughly assess the problem before you propose any solutions.

It's really just problem-solving 101: in order to figure out what to do, you need to determine what you're trying to solve. If you know you want to reach a certain future state, the goal is to figure out the best method to get there. The Find stage is the key to uncovering the best method to reach your organization's goals. It may not be A + B + C + D, because even though the **FUEL** process creates a framework, the stages are not always linear, as you'll see in the example in the next section below.

Through the **FUEL** process, you may start out focusing on what looks on the surface to be the biggest gap, but then, through analysis, discover that the area you've identified as the source of the problem is not the problem at all. In some cases, companies know something is wrong, but they don't have the right name for it—and thus end up labeling it a "communications" problem or a "time management" problem, when those things may have nothing to do with what's actually gone wrong.

BECOMING A SCIENTIST OF YOUR OWN BUSINESS

If you're having trouble imagining how the Find stage might help your company, this real-world example can help you recognize the power of digging deeper before trying to solve problems:

A mid-size company that I work with had made significant progress over the past two years toward some preliminary goals that we'd set together, but then hit some new roadblocks and became stuck again. Some of the problems were related to the evolution of a different reporting structure that I'd helped the leadership team put in place in my early work with them.

To be specific, their customer service group had started reporting to their director of sales, because previously when the group reported to the general manager, they didn't feel like they were getting enough respect. So the management team got together and tried to figure out what to do about the problem. But everyone else had too much on their plate already, so by default, the director of sales became the person to whom the customer service team reported.

Though this change meant the team now reported to someone who clearly respected them more, it now led to several new problems. For one, because the sales director traveled frequently, he was not available for the customer service team to access on a day-to-day basis. Then there was the fact that he didn't like conflict, so he tried to avoid getting in the middle, brushing team concerns aside in an effort to try to move on more quickly—to be fair, he was paid by commission to close deals; he was not paid to solve team problems.

Without someone on top of the details on a regular basis, as the general manager had been, the team started making more mistakes, so the company brought in a controller to direct the team's day-to-day concerns, even though the sales director still directed their activities. So although the addition of a new person in the mix solved one problem, by having someone more available to the team, it created another: confusion about who the team really reported to. When there was a conflict, who would stage in for the tie breaker?

I re-joined the leadership team in meetings to try to solve these newly emerging problems, as well as to discuss strategy about where the president wanted the organization to go over the next two years. The company had some realistic growth strategies, yet the leadership team had not firmly grasped the fact that they were facing potential risk factors from these situations that could put their growth goals in jeopardy. The company had made a huge investment not only in equipment, but in personnel, so doing the wrong thing might not break them, but it could stall them, and they might miss an opportunity.

In a desperate moment in one of these meetings, the president turned to me and asked, "Mary, can't you just write me a proposal?" And I remember thinking, "No, I don't want to write you a proposal, because it would just be another band-aid." The company had already tried band-aids, which got them to a certain level, but then they became stuck.

Despite their problems, the customer service team had moved ahead to a level that the rest of the organization had not. The team had been empowered, but the rest of the organization was still stuck in the old culture. A suggestion was made to train the rest of the organization to raise them up to the same level of knowledge. The president agreed—but the general manager wasn't on board.

This may seem like a lot of specific details to share with you, but these are the essence of the Find stage. You have to roll up your sleeves and see where the problems, conflicts, and gaps really are. And you have to be willing to be honest about them, even if it means you can't solve things linearly. In this case, though it certainly would have made my job easier to just say yes to the president's request to write a new proposal, it would have only provided a temporary solution, and it wouldn't have helped the company reach its two-year growth goals.

So my advice to this leadership team, although difficult for all involved, was that the company should go back to the beginning and assess their needs anew—it was a "when in hole, stop digging" recommendation. Though the company had made a lot of progress in the last few years toward the goals that we'd originally established together, the latest Find stage revealed that continuing to push forward in the same direction was no longer the best strategy. The situation had changed, and the strategy needed to change accordingly.

This organization needed to go back to the drawing board and ask:

> Now that we know what our needs are—
>
> Now we've done our needs assessment and we have our needs analysis—
>
> Now that we know where we want to go—
>
> Now that we have evolved to this stage—
>
> —where does our performance gap lie?

The Find stage is all about that: you're just playing detective using the marketplace, opportunities, and resources you might have. It's about becoming a scientist of your own business, understanding all of the factors involved (both good and bad), finding out where your gap is, and then continuing to track that gap over time as the company evolves.

Here's the take-home:

> *The Find stage is about pushing aside the immediate reaction that says, "Let's throw a solution at it." Instead, it's about training yourself and your leadership team to ask, "How did we get here?" If you can take the time to dig beneath the surface of apparent problems and understand the factors behind them, then you can figure out the performance gaps you need to address in your organization—as well as the best way to address them in the next stage of FUEL.*

CHAPTER 12

PLUGGING YOUR PERFORMANCE GAPS BY UTILIZING YOUR RESOURCES

Once you reach the Utilize stage, the question turns from "What's wrong?" to "What resources do we have available to fix it?" If the Find stage is about discovery, the Utilize stage is about action plans. The whole point of "Find" is to uncover performance gaps that are causing productivity to lag in your company. "Utilize" helps you plug those gaps, ideally using in-house resources that may be sitting right in front of you.

This next stage involves figuring out the best ways to use your existing resources to tackle the problems you've identified. Or, if you discover in "Find" that you are lacking internal resources in certain areas, strategizing other ways to fill those needs.

In terms of the big picture, here's what this stage looks like:

- You take everything you've learned in stage one and use it to guide your strategic decisions around your problem areas.
- You map everything out, asking yourself, "Now that we know what we're *lacking*, what do we *have* that we can utilize to solve these challenges?"
- You survey your internal resources, which might involve deploying your employees, your managers, or even your vendors toward solving certain problems. For challenges you can't solve in-house, you consider third-party solutions.

Maybe during the Find stage, you learned that although you hired great people, you lack the capacity to get the job done. The goal of "Utilize" then becomes figuring out what is mission-critical, and what can be outsourced or pushed down and out to other areas or functions.

The whole process can take a while and shouldn't be rushed. You might decide to pick some low hanging fruit now as you move toward your corporate problem-solving initiatives. You can then go back later, continuing to ask, "Now where are we at?" as you inch closer to your goal: the future state you've identified by doing your homework in "Find."

The "bridge" between these two stages can be emphasized when you consider the concept of "approach and deployment". In the 1990's, many organizations hared off down the route of "Total Quality" and would learn about such ideas as Quality Circles, or Continuous Improvement Teams and bosses would say they had to have them. That's all well and good, but management would often see that they'd implemented the "approach" and think that's all they had to do—wrong.

There was also critical need to make sure such initiatives were embedded into the psyche of the organization—i.e. they were fully deployed—otherwise they were likely to just wither and die. Find and Utilize can be viewed the same way here, in terms of making sure theoretical organizational strengths really are that in reality. You might think you have a brilliantly worded vision for your business, but can every employee relate their job to it? In the next section I'll talk about a great process that wasn't.

CURBING CORNER-CUTTING

The point is that Utilize is where companies should be spending most of their time, yet many leaders like to cut corners at this stage. That's not a good idea. Taking the path of least resistance now will likely come back to bite you down the road, in the form of decreased profits or even the failure of your organization.

To help explain why, let's start by examining a basic practice that is integral to corporate success: hiring. When I help companies through the **FUEL** process, I'm always surprised by how many haven't taken the time to put their ducks in a row by putting key organizational building blocks in place: mission and vision statements, core values, organizational charts, and job descriptions. Companies may have grown to nearly 100 employees, yet when I ask them if they have an org chart or job descriptions for their positions, the answer is, "Kind of…sort of…no."

You may think of these elements as nice but unnecessary—they're not. They're critical to what happens next in your business. They provide the framework and guidance you need to do the right things and hire the right people depending on the corporate goals you've set. Skipping the step of creating them is a shortcut that makes for a long delay. Not deploying them effectively makes things even worse.

As well as being able to challenge assumed strengths, this is another reason that the Find stage is so important, because you really do find out about a lot that's missing that can easily be resolved once you reach "Utilize." It's easy enough to write a job description, even if you decide to hire someone else to do it—but how can you expect to hire the best candidate for a particular position if you haven't really defined what the job is?

Utilize for your hiring process begins with something as simple as job descriptions, because even customized strategies won't work if you don't have the right people in place to accomplish your goals. If you don't have job descriptions, how do you expect to hire the right people?

So if a company is having problems with engagement and productivity, I want to see their job descriptions in the Find stage. If we discover they have no formal job descriptions, then the Utilize stage becomes directed at figuring out how to solve that problem, first examining in-house resources before considering outsourcing. It can be as simple as asking, "Who can create the necessary job descriptions to ensure the right candidates are targeted for the job?"—and then providing an answer that gets the job done.

MAPPING IT OUT

Here's something else that's important to know about the Utilize stage. When you notice a gap in knowledge from your work in "Find," this deficit might exist because you're lacking certain resources in-house—in these cases it makes sense to call for help from outside your company. But in many cases, the gap only exists because someone hasn't sat down and mapped the process out to figure out what's going on. This is where a process flow chart can really come in handy.

When I first start working with a company in the Find stage, I ask team members to map out certain key processes using flow charts or a "value stream map" to get an idea of where the bottlenecks are. For example, for a sales organization, I might ask the sales team to trace how an order becomes an order, and the sequence of steps the order takes throughout the entire operation from start to finish. I often discover standard processes like this have never been formally mapped out. How do you make improvements at the Utilize stage if you don't even know basic facts like how an order becomes an order?

Even if everyone on the team thinks they know the process, it's of limited value if no one has written the correct process down. Once you write it down and you can see it in living color on a flow chart, and people are often surprised about what's really involved in getting from A to B—"It takes that many steps to go here?" Everyone only knows their own little slice of the pie, but they don't know the full recipe.

I recommended flow charts for a mid-size company that was having trouble with purchase orders. If you had asked the managers if everyone followed the same process to create an order, they would have said "yes" unanimously and with confidence—they had a really good process. But when we started to map it out step by step, we didn't get very far in the process when we realized everyone followed a slightly different procedure. It was nowhere near as good as management thought.

We found out that someone put notes in one section and someone put notes in another section, and another person didn't put notes in at all. Someone printed out every single email and attached them to the file, and someone else just summarized the email. The mapping-out process begins in "Find," but in "Utilize," it becomes about asking, "How can we easily fix this problem?" "How can we make this process really stick?"

In this case, the managers realized that when a small client didn't have a purchase order, many times it became a bottleneck because the client didn't know how to create one. As a solution, the company decided to provide their clients with a generic purchase order template, opting to pay an outside vendor for software rather than creating a template themselves. So they solved the problem just by mapping out the whole process, seeing where the pain was, considering their in-house and third-party options, and utilizing resources they had at their disposal to solve it.

YOU DON'T ALWAYS NEED A CONSULTANT

It might be surprising to hear a consultant say that you don't always need a consultant, but I'm just "keeping it real," as they say. Though it's not always in my best interests, I often recommend that companies look internally first to utilize their own resources before bringing in a third party to solve the problems unearthed by "Find."

While a consultant might be helpful and might be the right choice under certain circumstances, you don't always have to turn to someone on the outside. You might want to look at your own people first and try to determine who wants a chance to solve the problem using resources you already have.

I've worked with many companies tackling process changes, and when they surveyed their internal resources, they found hands raised by employees who said, "I'd love to be part of that." If you've got people who are willing to do it, it's often smart to take them up on it—as corporate insiders they have more behind-the-scenes knowledge about particular pieces of your business than a third party could have.

Everyone in your company is the "master of their domain" about some aspect of your business, and that makes your employees and your managers valuable trainers for the rest of your workforce. Why hire a third party if you have the expertise under your own roof to get the job done? If you're smart (and budget conscious), you'll tap these individuals as the ones to help create job aids or training materials, partnering with learning consultants only as needed. If you have a subject matter expert who knows a lot about a piece of software, it might make sense for him or her to train others in it.

Drawing on internal resources during the Utilize phase can help keep you and perhaps your top team from drowning in minutia as well. Instead of you personally rolling up your sleeves and coming to the rescue again, your people can become the engine that helps create and generate tailored training opportunities. The challenge is ensuring that their schedules really allow them to take on these projects on top of their regular workload. If they start falling behind from a productivity standpoint or start making errors, then the exercise is counter-productive.

Even vendors can add value as knowledge banks and resource providers. Consider asking vendors to provide training on such as new materials they're involved with. In the process of sharing what they know with your teams, the interaction with your staff will help vendors understand more about the people using their products and materials, what their needs are, and the process as a whole. Questions can be answered up front before obstacles are encountered, saving everyone from future headaches.

Other businesses can also serve as resources if you're able to identify and articulate the mutual value of a partnership. As long as a business isn't a competitor, it might prove a valuable alliance for creation of a cohort, user group, or roundtable. My favorite bit of benchmarking was when a tourism business visited a prison to see how they managed people in line! So get creative in the Utilize stage, and expand your thinking about how to build a better business using the tools at your fingertips.

SAVING MONEY BY FOREGOING SPOON-FEEDING

Some leadership teams want to be spoon-fed their training information. If you're not among them, you can save a bundle. I knew a consultant who turned reading a book into a three-year engagement with a company that preferred to have someone else read and analyze for them. The CEO of the company wanted to train his company to use the principles in a popular management book, but everyone was too busy to read the book themselves.

So instead, the consultant bought the book, broke the lessons down into bite-size pieces, and created a workbook out of it to deliver to all employees. The consultant would be flown in to conduct a session on one chapter and lead a discussion about it. That's a good gig, because if you think about it, this company had access to the same resources that the consultant did. Anyone could have bought the book, read it themselves, and learned everything there was to know about it. In this case, spoon-feeding helped the company accomplish its goals, but they could have been accomplished by utilizing in-house resources as well.

If you want to keep your teams free to focus on their priorities without the distraction of additional training assignments, then you hire a third party. But be aware that most consultants have access to some of the same materials that you do. If you have internal resources who can manage these materials, you might save yourself the expense of a long engagement.

Here's another true story of how forward-thinking companies can take on more of the responsibility for internal training themselves at the Utilize stage and save themselves from incurring ongoing consulting fees:

I worked with a mid-sized company to help strengthen team communication among its leadership team and tighten evolving processes companywide by administering *Insights Discovery*®. Once our initial work together was completed, the company asked me about providing the same type of ongoing training to their new hires.

It certainly would have been a great opportunity for me, but I was aware that the company also had internal resources they could draw upon to reach similar results to those they would have reached by continuing to work with me as an outside consultant. Although recommending this strategy undercut my own business, I frankly felt it would be best for them to get certified in Insights themselves so that they could start delivering the training internally to their new hires.

I think it's important for all companies to look at their own internal resources before they come to me, or to any third party. It's my goal to help nudge companies to the point where they grow and begin dealing with other issues beyond what they started out with. The decisions that leaders make in "Utilize" give companies that chance.

So although I could have become this company's "new hires" person, I instead gave them the option to "utilize" their HR person by getting her certified in Insights. For a similar financial investment at the outset, they could either bring me in every time to train their new hires, or they could invest in learning the training to deliver it themselves.

By going "DIY" in your training efforts, though it may cost slightly more out of pocket initially to get certified, there's an additional advantage: it becomes a perpetual skill set to draw on in your organization. If your company decides on an in-house option like this, you can repeat the training over and over again as many times as needed without having to call for outside help. This would become a significant cost saving over time.

So my recommendation to all companies in the Utilize stage is, see what you can do on your own first—maybe you need a third party, and maybe you don't. But don't assume that you do.

USING THE RIGHT TOOLS

As you can see from the examples above, a big part of the Utilize stage involves not just filling gaps with any old resources, but figuring out the best resources to get a particular job done. Here's another example:

I spoke with a company once that said they actually still used classified ads to post jobs. My first thought was, how many people look for jobs in the classifieds? And my second thought was, what is the quality of those job seekers compared to the ones using more targeted online job boards? Are the classifieds really where you want your target market coming from?

Just to be sure I was right about my hunch, I followed up by going to the classifieds to look at the job listings, just to see what kind of information you get there. The answer is, not much: since the postings are paid by the word, the goal is to try to be as brief as possible. Generally you'll see the name of the company, the job title, and a little bit of information about the responsibilities and benefits. If this is all that you are providing to prospective applicants, it's no wonder you've got turnover in your business: you're hiring from the classifieds without a proper job description!

This also connects to the earlier point about avoiding short cuts. Not only is where you post your job important to reach your target market, but what you say in your job ad is also important. How effective is it to post a job in the classifieds—or on a job board for that matter—if you don't even have an internal job description that clearly describes what the position is? You have to put some effort in on the front end of your hiring process if you want to get quality applicants targeted to what you need. Doing so helps cut down on turnover and saves your business money.

With the job-search and candidate-search technologies available today, there's no reason to miss out on the opportunity to truly target the candidates you want. Some sites even have analytics to help you place your job ad in front of the exact people who might be looking for your type of job.

When it comes to selecting the best tools for your goals, that's a classic utilization opportunity. Don't utilize the classified ads in your local paper—that's poor utilization. While it may cost you a little more on the front end than less effective options, working with a more targeted job board helps you get in front of the right people, which will likely lead to a better quality hire.

USING SIX SIGMA

I have one more way to help you think about the Utilize stage: by comparing it to how Toyota interprets Six Sigma quality control and their strategic approach to improvements. The Robert E. Nolan Company defines Six Sigma as:

> *"A disciplined, data-driven approach and methodology for eliminating defects in any process—from manufacturing to transactional and from product to service."*

And from Wikipedia:

> *Six Sigma seeks to improve the quality of the output of a process by identifying and removing the causes of defects and minimizing variability in manufacturing and business processes. It uses a set of quality management methods, mainly empirical, statistical methods, and creates a special infrastructure of people within the organization, who are experts in these methods. Each Six Sigma project carried out within an organization follows a defined sequence of steps and has specific value targets, for example: reduce process cycle time, reduce pollution, reduce costs, increase customer satisfaction, and increase profits*

When Toyota designs a car, they immediately start thinking about how they can improve it—and they've been doing that for decades. Toyota was manufacturing cars back in the 1970s when you wouldn't be caught dead driving a Japanese car. Today, thanks to the quality controls put in place by car manufacturers like Toyota using Six Sigma, you see more foreign cars on the road than American cars. That's how far Toyota came up in quality, perception, and reputation by using their own form of the Utilize stage.

If you think about it, the real reason for Toyota's success is that they've continued to improve incrementally over time, to the point where the only things left to tinker with are the bells and whistles. The improvement engineers at Toyota now are working on elements like the O ring of the cigarette lighter, or the buttons on the radio, or materials for floor mats. That's where they're at today, because their cars are running perfectly.

This should be your goal as well—to solve problems so efficiently by smart utilization of your resources that the engagement level in your company becomes and remains high, and your leadership team continuously supports the mission, vision, and goals of your organization. And that leads us right into the final two stages of **FUEL**: Engage and Lead.

Here's the take-home:

> *The Utilize stage requires that you get creative and expansive in your thinking about how to build a better business. Once you've identified performance gaps in the Find stage, the real work begins as you start to determine the best solutions. Many solutions can come from in-house, if you take the time to map out processes and truly understand them. There's no need to turn to a third party for training tools if you can tap willing parties within your own organization, or perhaps with your vendors or other non-competitor businesses.*

CHAPTER 13
RALLYING YOUR TROOPS FOR ENGAGEMENT

Let's start off this chapter by dispelling again the biggest myth about employee engagement. That's the one that tells company owners that having happy or satisfied employees means that they have an engaged workforce. Nothing could be further from the truth. Just because you have a satisfied employee base does not mean that they're engaged.

I once had a job where I could have sat back and done the bare minimum all day long. No one knew where I was or what I was doing, and no one cared. I was just collecting a paycheck. My boss lived three states away, and she had 1,001 other things on her plate to worry about. She had a boss who micromanaged her, so she spent all of her time jumping through hoops.

I could have given this boss the status quo, never stretching or growing in the position, and she would have been perfectly fine with my performance. Though the job wasn't fulfilling my desire to be challenged, I initially felt happy in it. For a while, I felt like, "Great! I'm getting paid to do nothing!" That feeling didn't last, because eventually, I wanted more from the position than it could provide me. But there were some appealing things about the job that could have very easily kept me stuck in it.

In fact, if you had sent me an employee engagement survey back then asking if I was satisfied with that job, I probably would have said yes. I was highly compensated. My boss loved me. I could do what I wanted. I felt generally satisfied.

If the survey had asked, "Does your boss provide you with adequate direction?" I might have answered, "Yeah, she leaves me the hell alone. I like that." If it had asked, "Are you clear about what your roles and responsibilities are?" I'm sure I would have said, "Yep, 100 percent clear." I could have easily answered "yes" all the way down the line with questions like those, and I would have been considered a highly satisfied employee based on that survey. Based on the questions and my answers to them, it sounded like I was satisfied.

But the job itself was not satisfying to me, and that's the difference. It didn't make me "love" my employer and, for example, I had no interest in trying to drive improvements. If I had done that I'd have done myself out of a job!

NO PACKAGE DEAL

Here's a related point you'll want to remember before you start surveying your own employees for their level of engagement: *you can be happy at work and do a horrible job.* As happened to me, you might be in a job that pays well, and because your manager sucks and doesn't push you into making decisions, you can be late on projects. Feeling this "freedom," you might feel perfectly happy and perfectly satisfied. But that does not mean you're engaged and giving your top performance.

An engaged employee fires on all cylinders, and doesn't leave anything in the tank at the end of the day, because he or she gives it all to you. They don't hold back on giving you 100 percent because they believe that your company's success is their own success. They are tuned in to what's going on strategically in your company, and they understand your initiatives and your customers.

It doesn't matter whether your business is selling plastic or pharmaceuticals—if this employee is on board with your mission, and excited about it, that's when you have someone who's engaged. This employee might even be satisfied and happy as well as engaged—but those qualities are not all created equal, and don't always come as a package deal.

FUELING ENGAGEMENT

With that general backdrop on what employee engagement is and isn't, let's now examine how the **FUEL** process relies on the Engage stage. A good way to do that is through an example of an engaged team. This will motivate you to want to reach this stage as quickly as possible—and I'll show you how to do that at the end of the chapter.

I like to think of the Engage stage as a rally cry: "This is what we have to accomplish; what do you guys think?" Everybody gets a chance to chime in and be a part of it. Everyone feels like they're being brought into the picture. It's not a top-down approach; it's very collaborative. It's *their* change as much as much as it's yours.

The beauty of this system is that most people don't argue with their own data, especially when it's generated in a group. So the more you can create ownership of the changes among your employees, the better it's going to be and result in full-team support for the ideas, and it "self-corrects" if someone doesn't play along.

I once worked on a really well engaged team, where we were tasked with helping to provide customer service training for the rest of the organization. There was only one catch—we had no budget. As engaged employees, we cared about solving this problem together, so we asked ourselves, much as companies do in the Utilize stage, who do we have to help us with this? We checked in with our sales training and manufacturing training departments, asking what kind of content did they have and what things were they doing, and unearthed training materials that people forgot existed.

When teams are engaged, they pull out all the stops to help each other reach a solution. Everyone takes on tasks willingly. We had people on our team who wracked their brains and said, "You know what? I remember so-and-so running a customer service course over in the call center." Even though the call center customer service approach was somewhat different than what we were trying to do in our department, it still gave us a great starting point from which to launch our training.

True to the learnings of the Utilize stage, we didn't stop with our in-house resources, and approached some of our vendors as well. We let them know that while we couldn't buy materials since we had no budget, we would love to borrow their resources and pay them back later, through an internal charge-back system.

Someone on our team had an idea to take this a step further by holding a vendor fair. We invited everyone and anyone we thought could be involved in a solution to our problem, and asked them to come and show off their materials that might help us accomplish our goals. We invited the vendors to ask questions about our problem, and they did. Even though there was no budget and no immediate or guaranteed financial gain for anyone if they helped us, it was a true collaboration with everyone focused around our particular problem. I can't tell you motivational it was and we all became even more engaged.

COLLABORATIVE SPIRIT

The amazing part about this full-team engagement, which included both internal and external players, was that vendors went so far as to point us to free resources that they would otherwise have charged for. They were engaged enough that they were willing to give supplies away and other vendors offered people resources—maybe lunch with their instructional designer who could share some ideas.

The collaborative spirit grew and grew. As vendors saw their competitors willing to throw in something, they became willing, too. It became clear that the help was mutually beneficial—by sharing their internal resources, they were not only assisting us in our mission; they were helping themselves as well.

Vendors even started piggybacking on each other's solutions, saying, "Well if they're going to do that, then I've got this resource that can help you create the actual materials." People recognized that it made sense to work together, because if we created a customer service course that fulfilled all our ideas and needs then they could really use it as well.

In the end, we were able to take what we already had in-house as a starting point—training from the call center—and build upon it through free services from our vendors. The result was the creation of a definitive, companywide customer service training guide to use whether members of staff were on the phone or in the field.

HOW TO APPROACH THE ENGAGE STAGE

By the time you've reached the Engage stage, you've completed your research and you know what problem you're actually seeking to solve. You're also committed to ensuring that you don't just throw some off-the-shelf, open-ended program at the problem, hoping it's going to work. The Engage level is about knowing it's working, and having everyone on board.

As you saw from the above example, this stage means that you:

- Recognize (through the Find stage) that you have certain competencies, yet you're aware that there are competencies that still need to be filled;
- Identify (through the Utilize stage) some training that you can do and technical resources that are available;
- Bring those things together and share them with your team—the goal now (through the Engage stage) is to have both your managers and your employees willing to do whatever it takes through full engagement to reach your goals.

But how do you actually ensure that your teams are engaged and not just coasting along in a satisfied but uninspired way? That's where the customization comes in that I keep talking about. What spells engagement at my company might not spell engagement at yours. And as we saw in the example above of my personal bout of disengagement, a generic employee survey may ask the wrong questions of your employees and thus deliver false results.

While leaders often hope for best practices when it comes to engagement, there aren't any. So it's up to you to measure your own employees' engagement rather than comparing your organization to other companies. You need to find out what *your* employees value—and what true engagement looks like to them—before you can design the right measurement tool for your specific workforce.

What motivates the hearts and minds of your most important assets for propelling your company forward? Once you've determined that, these engagement-related measurements are crucial to determining the exact direction in which to tailor your development initiatives, with the aim of ensuring that your whole company is rallying behind you.

Becoming aware of the current state of engagement is not enough, however. Engaged employees today may not be engaged employees tomorrow. Once you've accurately measured current engagement, you need to develop ways to keep employees engaged in the future. This involves ensuring that you fully understand what was making them engaged in the first place, and then being equally sure that you are maintain that as well as experimenting with different methods of harnessing the energy and excitement of the entire organization for the long haul. Again, this process *must* be customized to *your* people to have real and long-lasting value.

Here's the take-home:

> *Having satisfied—or even happy—employees doesn't mean you have engaged employees. Happy employees can be completely disengaged from your company's mission and do a terrible job.*
>
> *The goal of the Engage stage is to have both your managers and your employees willing to do whatever it takes through full engagement to reach your goals. Engaged teams pull out all the stops to help reach a solution together. They rally internal and external resources, with a collaborative spirit that builds strength from the bottom-up.*
>
> *Customization is crucial in measuring employee engagement. There are no accurate best practices for determining engagement, and generic surveys can deliver false results. You need to know what your employees value in order to design the right measurement tool for your specific workforce. What gets measured gets done, so these engagement-related measurements are crucial to effectively determine the best direction for your development initiatives.*

CHAPTER 14

BRINGING IT ALL FULL CIRCLE FOR EFFECTIVE LEADERSHIP

"I'm convinced that every major problem we face as a country is a leadership problem."

—**Jim Collins**, Author, *Good to Great*

That's a great quote, and it most certainly applies to the corporate world. I believe all problems faced in business can also be traced back to poor leadership. No matter what type of challenge we look at in any organization—whether communication, trust, or lack of engagement—if you trace the problem back to its origin, you'll find a problem with leadership at the end of the line.

That's why **FUEL** culminates with the Lead stage. Many corporate leaders and business managers make the mistake of trying to begin at the ending point of the **FUEL** process. They've stepped into a new leadership role, and they're ready to "start leading." Such leaders attempt jumping in with both feet, ready to make their mark on their team, division, and company.

However, there's a good reason why we've saved "Lead" for the final stage of **FUEL** rather than as its launching pad. That's because until you have diligently tackled the first three stages:

- Doing research to determine what problems need solving in the Find stage;
- Making the most of all available resources (including those in-house) to plug those performance gaps at the Utilize stage;
- Working with a customized solution to maximize true engagement in both your managers and employees at the Engage stage—you aren't ready to be an effective leader.

DON'T DIVE INTO LEAD TOO SOON

It may seem like there's a lot of work to do in the first three stages before you can get down to the business of leading—and there is. I'm not suggesting that you can't begin some basic work in influencing the leadership team, employees, and the culture of the organization as you work through the first three stages of the process, but tread warily.

What I'm saying is that it's a mistake to try to be an effective leader without first finding out what the organization needs. You need to first direct your energy and creativity into determining the best resources to utilize to solve specific problems, and using customization to measure and develop employee engagement. But the good news is, while much work precedes true preparedness for great leadership, the Lead stage itself becomes very straightforward in the wake of those earlier efforts.

The Find, Utilize, and Engage stages are all about what must be done to prepare for the Lead stage. "Lead" thus becomes more about what you *don't* need to do rather than about taking specific action. It's more of an "anti-stage" if you will, and that's because, ideally, if you've completed each of the preliminary stages, there isn't anything to *do*, per se, in the Lead stage except empower others to do their jobs and get out of the way. Your work on the front end of **FUEL** should make the actual act of leadership much easier.

Once you have a solid grasp of where your development gaps are and have addressed those gaps while engaging people around each limitation, it becomes simply a matter of leading your team, and continuing with any pre-identified strengths. You won't need to focus on identifying or fixing problems for them—you've already done your work to pave the way for their success.

By the time you reach the Lead stage, it becomes more about ongoing listening to your team's ideas on what they think they can do to keep moving forward toward the company's goals, based on the findings from the first three stages of **FUEL**. It's about saying, "Okay, go do that!"

When you think about it, that's what great leadership is based on—encouraging others to be courageous and take bold steps. Strong leaders let their teams know that some stumbling is expected and accepted; it is better to try something innovative and do it wrong than to stay stuck safely in one place.

Effective leadership boils down to giving others what they need to go do it—to get out there even if moving forward means taking baby steps to come up with the best solution. So for leaders, a big part of the Lead stage of **FUEL** is just learning to step back and encourage trial and error.

IMAGINE "WHAT IF?"

There's another important aspect to the Lead stage as well. By the time you reach this final stage in the process, your role as a leader also must involve going back and re-envisioning the company. That's because if you've properly gone through Find, Utilize, and Engage, then your company will have inevitably changed by the time you get to Lead. Some leaders, upon recognizing that positive change has occurred, will be tempted to break their forward momentum in this heady moment of initial success. They may say, "Great, I've got the company I've always wanted," and stop evolving.

If you take this approach, then eventually, all of the effort you spent on the front end will be wasted, since a company is an organic entity, not a static one. The place you arrive at after your first round of "FUE" stages is not your ultimate destination, but merely a steppingstone on the company's path to continuous improvement—if you choose wisely at stage four. Also liken your company to a smooth running engine—you can't only put FUEL in once.

Successful leaders understand that they can't perpetuate the same thing over and over again. If in doubt, reread Chapter 3 on "Why You Can't Manage Change." As a quick refresher, the process of navigating organizational change is not a straightforward A + B = C. It's A + B initially, and then you reevaluate based on that output.

The **FUEL** process recognizes that when you reach the Lead stage, it's not about saying, "Good! Check! Done!" While you can certainly pat yourself on the back for the progress made to date, now is not the time to rest on your laurels. Instead, the Lead stage provides the opportunity to go back and look at the entire organization and its challenges with fresh eyes, because it's not the same place that it was when you started back at stage one.

As a leader, you may be relieved to discover that the first three "FUE" stages have resulted in the company you've always wanted—but the best leaders will recognize that this isn't enough. They will say, "Now, let's make it *even* better," and will begin to re-envision the company as they evaluate and identify areas for additional growth.

RE-FUEL—A RE-ENVISIONING EXERCISE

In one sense, the re-envisioning process of Lead is similar to the detective-playing that you did in the Find stage—but it isn't exactly the same. It's no longer in the realm of that initial identification to unearth all of the problems and gaps that exist in your organization. By now, those initial issues have either been resolved or are "works in progress," moving toward repair via previously selected solutions. So Lead instead becomes about turning it up a notch and seeking continuous improvement over time. It becomes about asking such as:

- What if you I every employee, every customer, every vendor, and every manager in lockstep with each other?
- What if great customer service was not an exception, but the norm, because my teams are just that good?
- What if all of my team's processes were in sync with every other division's?

But these are merely examples for the book, and your actual "what if" questions may very well differ depending on what's important to your company, and what problems still need to be solved. Remember, "off-the-shelf" solutions don't work, so stay in the mind of customizing this stage to your organization's unique situation and where it is in your cycles of growth.

To practice this exercise, simply imagine that your company is now the company you knew you'd have after identifying and addressing performance gaps, as well as identifying the best way to solve corporate problems utilizing your resources. You have everybody on board—in fact, everyone's not only reading the same book from the same page, but they're all reading in unison. What would that look like—and more importantly at the Lead stage, what comes next? As a leader, what will you do for an encore to keep this forward momentum going and going and going?

"Lead" is about figuring out what "up a notch" from your new norm would look like, and re-envisioning what you had envisioned three, four, or five years ago when you began the **FUEL** process. As the company grows, effective leaders need to evolve with it and look at it differently based on each new iteration. As with the engine again, the time to re-FUEL is always going to come around.

The truly effective leader is the person who continuously coordinates the iterative **FUEL** process. He or she recognizes that there is a performance problem—or an opportunity for improvement—and initiates the **FUEL** process again. Working with the team, they determine when each stage has been effectively achieved and gets agreement to launch the next step. He or she continuously empowers their team to go through the stages with the necessary encouragements, prodding and positive reinforcement, ensuring they measure progress while thinking of the next iteration cycle.

As we come to the end of describing the **FUEL** process, it's important to look back and see how far we've journeyed. We've talked about why most existing leadership development doesn't work, and explored the heavy costs of using training and development programs that are misdirected. We've walked through what you need to start doing, stage by stage, to **FUEL** your organization to the next level. Now it's a matter of "go do it."

If you want a better business, then you have to *build* a better business, taking baby steps that result in small improvements over time. The answers won't be found in elaborate solutions where one size fits none—you can only make it happen by going back to the basics, doing the work, and continuously evolving.

Here's the take-home:

The Lead stage brings the other three stages of FUEL full circle, resulting in more effective leadership and an environment of continuous improvement.

While many leaders try to start with this last stage, they can improve their leadership capabilities (and make their jobs easier) by first completing the Find, Utilize, and Engage stages. Those who do so will find that "Lead" becomes about stepping back and empowering others to get things done, while re-envisioning the company—which has changed dramatically through undergoing the first three stages—with fresh eyes.

The leaders who can continue asking "What if?" and then act on those answers will continue to evolve while keeping their companies competitive.

THE FINAL WORD

As you begin to work with your organization to sort out "what's gone wrong" with developing your leadership team and set about to right the ship, I encourage you to remember these key concepts about why most standard approaches to leadership development fail:

- When it comes time to choose your strategies for leadership development, it's best to avoid a "one-size-fits-all" approach. If training tools or courses haven't been designed to address your company's specific challenges, then their tactics won't effectively solve your problems.
- Employee engagement is about more than having satisfied, or even happy, employees—it's about creating a culture that encourages engagement rather than squelches it, and it starts even before you hire someone.

- No type of training can solve all of your organization's performance issues. Any training effort is futile if it's not tied to specific learning objectives that are relevant to *your* company alone.
- Certain types of challenges are inherently unmanageable, including change, time, and stress—but reactions to these challenges can and should be managed.
- You need to understand what's going on inside your organization in particular before you can determine how best to fix it. The key is to leave classic "training" behind, focusing instead on true development of competencies, skills, and behaviors needed for effective, authentic leadership.

Next, don't forget the serious negative business outcomes of taking the wrong approach to development, and ineffectively funneling your time and resources into areas that can't be fixed:

- There are high emotional costs to poor leadership development—specifically the low morale and high turnover that results from disengagement.
- These emotional costs trickle down to damage company productivity. Maximum benefit occurs only when your company's leadership development inspires *true* employee engagement that leads to better customer support, and ultimately increased productivity.
- At the end of this downward spiral is a hit to your company's bottom line. Suboptimal leadership practices can leave substantial sums on the table each year, leading to a drain in your company's financial performance.

Finally, here's a recap about the stages you can take to **FUEL** your organization to the next level:

- The **Find** stage is about becoming a scientist of your own business, understanding all of the factors involved (both good and bad), discovering where your gaps are, and then continuing to track those gaps over time. It's about digging beneath the surface of problems and understanding the factors behind them, and then you can figure out the performance issues you need to address in your organization.

- In the **Utilize** stage, the question turns from "What's wrong?" to "What resources do we have available to fix it?" Your goal at this stage is to determine the best solutions, whether in-house, with your vendors, or with a third party.

- The **Engage** stage is about knowing it's working, and having everyone on board. Ideally, by the time you complete this stage, you will have managers and employees alike willing to do whatever it takes to reach your goals. Customization is crucial in measuring employee engagement. You need to know what your employees value in order to design the right measurement tools for your specific workforce.

- The **Lead** stage brings the other three stages of **FUEL** full circle, resulting in more effective leadership and an environment of continuous improvement. "Lead" becomes about stepping back and empowering others to get things done, while continually re-envisioning the company with fresh eyes.

As you come to the end of the book, it's important to look back and see how far we've journeyed. We've talked about why most existing leadership development doesn't work, and explored the heavy costs of using training and development programs that are misdirected.

We've walked through what you need to start doing, step by step, to **FUEL** your organization to the next level . . . And now it's a matter of "go do it!"

Here's the final take home:

> *If you want a better business, then you have to build a better business, taking baby steps that result in small improvements over time. The answers won't be found in elaborate solutions where one size fits none—you can only make it happen by going back to the basics, doing the work, and continuously evolving.*
>
> *Believe in your business and seek to turn it into the smoothest running engine your particular market—and then keep on re-FUELing it.*

ABOUT THE AUTHOR

Mary's first foray into the world of writing was as one of the co-authors of "So What Do You Do?" with her mentor and New York Times best seller, Joel Comm. That experience really got her started and, as well as speaking, she started blogging and writing articles on personal development, leadership, organizational change and so on—her specialties for over 20 years that led to the birth of her company Ember Carriers in 2008.

Mary has driven highly successful change management and leadership development programs—that lead to increased profits and improved employee engagement—in numerous organizations of all shapes and sizes, and all that rich experience provided more content for her writing.

As she learned more and more about what works and what doesn't, she eventually decided to organize her rantings and write a book on her *What's Gone Wrong*™ thoughts about developing leaders in today's world.

Her goal was to create pertinent and applicable content that any leader could put to work immediately, whether they were a VP in a Fortune 500 company, or ran their own emerging enterprise. Best-selling author Ray Edwards believes she's succeeded, and she hopes that you do too.

As well as reading Mary's wisdom, you can also hear her speak. She's addressed audiences throughout North America and internationally, conducting workshops and providing keynotes for corporations, professional organizations and non-profit organizations. If you would like her to present at your next conference or convention, then please get in touch via bookmary@embercarriers.com.

www.embercarriers.com

www.whatsgonewrong.com

www.TheMorganJamesSpeakersGroup.com

We connect Morgan James published authors with live and online events and audiences whom will benefit from their expertise.

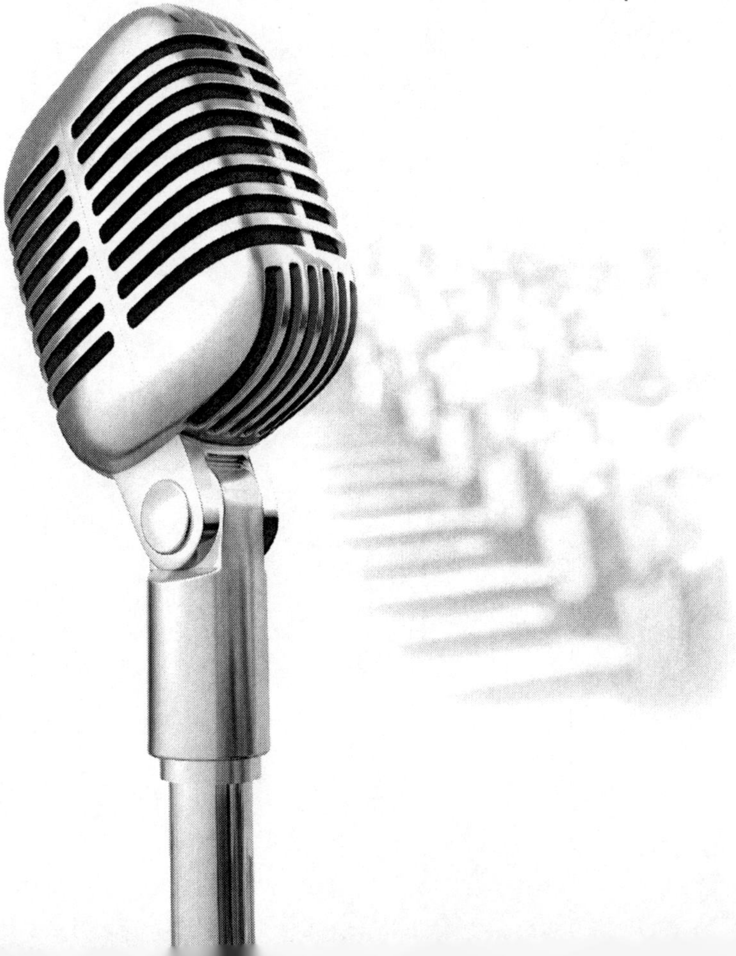

Morgan James makes all of our titles available through the Library for All Charity Organizations.

www.LibraryForAll.org

CPSIA information can be obtained
at www.ICGtesting.com
Printed in the USA
LVOW12s1834060717
540469LV00005B/909/P